Endc

With echoes of the genre of spiritual autobiography, Agnes Greene invites her readers to accompany her on a narrative journey through the most traumatic experience of her life, a journey from sickness to wellness, from faith to full faith. Along the path, the reader learns that this is not only Agnes Greene's story but also the story of close members of her family. It is the story of a family of one, for the different voices that help speak Agnes's story merge with her voice.

Afflicted with a brain tumor in March 1998, Agnes Greene's faith in God and in self is sorely but briefly tested, as is the faith of some of her family members. All pass the test with flying colors. Her narrative is indeed an uplifting story of the healing powers of faith, faith in the Lord Almighty and faith in the self. It is a story of the Love of God, the love of family, and the love of self. Readers who share in Agnes Greene's inspirational narrative of her journey should come away with a renewed awareness that Love can conquer all, and that God is Love.

J. Lee Greene
Professor of English, Emeritus
University of North Carolina at Chapel Hill

Seek and you shall find all the key ingredients in this book to weather any and all the challenges life can throw at you. The entire family's ability to show their strength and courage by implementing the Word of God as the source for all who reads this book is so amazing. My faith is renewed and I am forever blessed to be able to see the light through Agnes Greene's eyes. Victory is yours to claim, now and forever!

Tracy L. Durant-Walker, B.S., D.D.S.
A Quality Smile for You
Rock Hill, SC

This book is engaging, inspiring and compelling. Agnes Greene walks us through her miracle with clarity, conviction and a hint of humor that affords a gentle smile to cross you face. This book will challenge your faith, strengthen your commitment to the Lord and bring you to a place of acknowledgement of the awesomeness of our sovereign God.

Rev. Beverly Morrison-Caesar
Author, "Experiencing Your 25th Hour"
Bethel Gospel Tabernacle
Jamaica, NY

A near death experience on March 21, 1998, gave Agnes Greene a new revelation of just who God is and that she must relinquish complete control over to Him. Through her eyes and the eyes of her husband, children, sisters, other relatives and friends, they came to understand God's character, excellence, importance, and absolute power and control.

Agnes Greene has poured her heart into this book by telling of her valiant battle with brain cancer. She has used the memories of her family members to recount how they each came through this experience with her and how their faith was increased during the process. They all became witnesses to God's miracle working power. They saw how the prayers of many people were answered on Agnes's behalf.

Mrs. Greene saw family members transition from having an acquaintance with God to having an intimate relationship with Him. This experience opened their eyes to the wonders of God and in the words of Mrs. Greene, "God does all things well."

Janet Sims-Wood, Ph.D.
Oral Historian/Librarian/Bibliographer/Indexer

To read this book and embrace the contents within makes one appreciate the true character of God's almighty grace, mercy, faithfulness and the totality of His love for mankind.

Prophetess Patricia M. Currence
CEO, Weapons of Warfare International Prayer Ministry
Douglasville, Ga.

God Is Sovereign
i am nothing

My Diary of How God's Grace Saw Me through Brain Cancer

Agnes E. Greene

iUniverse, Inc.
New York   Bloomington

God is Sovereign, i am nothing
My Diary of How God's Grace Saw Me through Brain Cancer

iUniverse books may be ordered through booksellers or by contacting:

iUniverse
1663 Liberty Drive
Bloomington, IN 47403
www.iuniverse.com
1-800-Authors (1-800-288-4677)

For additional information and booking, contact:
Awesome God Group
1-888-640-2040
www.awesomeGODgroup.com

ISBN: 978-1-4502-1534-3 (sc)
ISBN: 978-1-4502-1536-7 (dj)
ISBN: 978-1-4502-1535-0 (ebk)

Printed in the United States of America

iUniverse rev. date: 5/17/2010

Dedication

This book is dedicated to my "yummy yummy" granddaughter, Gianni Alaina Greene (we call her GiGi). The gift of her life on March 10, 1998, brought a tremendous amount of joy to our family. Eleven days later, on March 21, I was graced with the gift of life, again—my own. GiGi gives me another reason to enjoy living.

Gianni, it is my prayer that you will continue to love and serve the God of Nana Agnes. I love you dearly!

Contents

Acknowledgments

I could not write this book without the Sovereign God—my Creator, my Savior, and my Comforter. So I simply want to say, "thank You Lord." I would also like to thank the many people who helped me, both during my illness and the writing process:

My precious husband and co-survivor—Jerry Greene

My darling children—Arnold and Tracey Greene

My delightful "second daughter"—Doneisha Tucker-Greene (Arnold's wife)

My birth family, the Gambles, especially my sisters—Saretter, Edna, Chars, Betty, Minnie, Ponzella, and Alphenia

My family by marriage, the Greenes, especially Geraldine and Terry

My "warring angel"—Rosie Sheard Parris

My "guardian angels"—Thelma Harty and Bettye Samuels

My "ministering angels"—Harry and Dawn Armand, Marjorie Canion, Robert and Winelle Crump, Pastor Marc Farmer, Pastor John Fortt, Pastor Charles Gill, Pastor Brenda Hazel, Rev. Pearl Hedgspeth, Gladys McFaddin and Rev. Clarence Howard (posthumously)

My "I'm here-for-you" friends—Elliot and Kathy Harrison and Vickie Dexter

Proofreaders—Gladys McFaddin, Wanda O'Neal-Beatle, Pearl Hedgspeth, and Melissa Strong

Graphic Artist—James G. Parris "Thank you for sharing your special gift"

Resident Editors—Pamela Toussaint and Tracey A. Greene

The entire iUniverse staff—I could not have done this without you!

My editorial consultant, Krista Hill—Thank you for everything. "You are the greatest!"

Foreword

I t is my profound privilege to introduce you to this powerfully insightful book and author. I have known Agnes E. Greene for over 40 years (most of my life) and have witnessed first-hand the exemplary life that she has led before God. This book surfaces only a minuscule portion of her life: but a portion that is grounded in the necessity of faith and most importantly God's sovereignty!

Hebrews 11:6 states "But without faith it is impossible to please him..." This scripture refers to the necessity for us to have undeniable faith in God. In other words, allowing the sovereignty of God to lead us down life's road when we may not agree with or understand the direction. This creates a vulnerability that is not comfortable for us. However, God does **ALL** things well and has an optimal destination and purpose for our lives. **God is Sovereign and I am nothing!**

This book takes you on a journey that many of us typically don't have the opportunity to experience. Elder Agnes (as I call her) is sharing with us some of the most intimate details of a tragic experience. Although, the details of this book may not correlate with what you have been through or will go through; the principle of this book and its lessons are applicable in all our lives. This book should inspire you to increase your faith in God and "rest" in his sovereignty. **God is Sovereign and I am nothing!**

There is a song I sing called "Stand." A verse in the song goes "... after you've done all you can, you just stand!" This song is analogous to what "Elder Agnes" writes about in this book as it relates to faith and God's sovereignty. Many times we experience things in our lives that leave us at a point where the best thing to do is to trust God and stand; knowing that God has never and will never fail. My friend, stand in the sovereignty of God. **God is Sovereign and I am nothing!**

I encourage you to read this book in its entirety. It will not only change your mindset but it will change your life. Enjoy this wonderful book and remember… **God is Sovereign and I am nothing!**

Donnie McClurkin
Gospel Music Recording Artist
and
Pastor of Perfecting Faith Church, Freeport, NY

Foreword from my "Co-Survivor"

While serving as a medic during the Vietnam War, I anxiously anticipated my first letter from "the States." Unbeknownst to me, the letter I received would alter the course of my life. I was expecting a love letter, but instead received a "Dear John" letter. Though I was heartbroken at the announcement, I knew my situation was not hopeless. Instead my faith leaped into action, as I prayed "God, from this day forward, I don't want another girlfriend. Please help me find my wife!" On October 4, 1969, God honored my prayer when I married the author of this book. Agnes is my wife, my best friend, my soul-mate, the mother of our children and the love of my life – 'til death do us part! She is my Proverbs 31 woman-full of creativity, moral strength and wisdom. Agnes is gifted to write, sing, teach and speak. She is accomplished at making wares with her hands. She has keen insight and the ability to conquer the challenge at hand. She shares her love and compassion with others, in an unselfish manner. She loves her family and meets the needs of our home. She has the utmost reverence for God-after all her name means "of God." Our children and grandchildren call her blessed. She is God's greatest gift to me and I pray you enjoy this gift that she shares with you.

Pastor Jerry A. Greene
Perfecting the Heart Worship Center
Chester, South Carolina

Introduction

Why God is sovereign and i am nothing

I realize it is a well-worn cliché, but March 21, 1998 was the first day of the rest of my life. The clock struck twelve thirty on the dawn of a new day. I didn't know it at the time, but the second stage of my journey on planet earth had just begun.

Much like the Old Testament character, Job, my family and I experienced a major crisis that shook our world, without any foreknowledge or forewarning. One minute, I was nestled in my bed "yakking" on the phone with a girlfriend, the next minute I was having a near-death experience. This crisis, and the events that followed, gave me a new understanding of who God is and who I am not. It is this revelation that provides the fuel for this book.

I know, I know, this book's title may be unsettling, and I commend you for pressing through this far! At a time when so many of our resources (time, money, and energy) are spent on discovering and developing "the self," declaring that "God is sovereign; i am nothing" may seem a bit out of sync with "modern Christianity." I am in no way opposed to having a better understanding of one's self or learning how to increase one's "market value" but I am convinced that, now more than ever, an authentic understanding of self must always be seen in light of the awesomeness of God's sovereignty. My desire is that as you read this book, you will see how God's sovereignty and my nothingness were always present yet never conflicting during this experience.

The great theologian A.W. Tozer gives a simple yet profound depiction of God's sovereignty:

> An ocean liner leaves New York bound for Liverpool. Its destination has been determined by proper authorities. Nothing can change it. On board the liner are several scores of passengers. These are not in chains, neither are their activities determined for them by decree. They are completely free to move about as they will. They eat, sleep, play, lounge about on the deck, read, talk, altogether as they please; but all the while the great liner is carrying them steadily onward toward a predetermined port.
>
> Both freedom and sovereignty are present here and they do not contradict each other. So it is, I believe, with man's freedom and the sovereignty of God. The mighty liner of God's sovereign design keeps its steady course over the sea of history. God moves undisturbed and unhindered toward the fulfillment of those eternal purposes which He purposed in Christ Jesus before the world began. We do not know all that is included in those purposes, but enough has been disclosed to furnish us with a broad outline of things to come and to give us good hope and firm assurance of future well-being.[1]

From childhood, I was taught that God is sovereign, and I had long accepted that concept. My father and mother were "God-fearing" Christians and they raised my siblings and me with a God consciousness. Grace was always said before meals; bedtime prayers were whispered before the lights were turned out. Cussing and swearing were out of the question (or certainly not done in their presence), and our father would pull out the gigantic family bible on Saturday nights and read those almost unbelievable stories to us. They never asked us if we wanted to attend church services; that was a given. I was taught that

God heard everything I said and saw everything I did, and even knew my thoughts before I could think them. And I believed that! So my overall understanding of God's sovereignty, from a young age, could best be described by the old song "He's Got the Whole World in His Hand." But it was the experience of March 21, 1998 and the ensuing months that God used to jump-start my journey of personally knowing His sovereignty. Webster defines sovereignty as: *being above all others in character, importance, excellence ... having absolute power and control.* The time had come for me to know God's character, God's importance, God's excellence, and God's absolute power and control. And I would soon come to know how those attributes related to little old me.

God's sovereignty and my nothingness are always juxtaposed, but they are not enemies. In fact, my nothingness is at one with God's sovereignty, through Jesus Christ. "For in Him [I] live, and move, and have [my] being ..." (Acts 17:28). It is God's sovereignty that enfolds (wraps up) and conceals (hides; covers or keeps from sight) my nothingness, and it is my nothingness that unfolds (spreads out or lays open to view) and exposes (presents to view; brings to light; unmasks) God's sovereignty. In other words, I could not exist today without God.

In the beginning, we were created in God's image and likeness (Genesis 1:26, 27). The image and likeness of God are revealed to us through His names and God's names reveal His character. God is Jehovah **Jireh**, my provider, when I have nothing. God is Jehovah **Shalom**, my peace, even when it seems my world is falling apart. God is Jehovah **Rophe**, my healer, even when the doctor says, "There's nothing else we can do." The circumstances in my life do not change who God is.

The acceptance of God's sovereignty and our nothingness is a concept that will be difficult for many to embrace—or even want to embrace. Because to do so, one has to recognize God's character, acknowledge God's importance, pattern God's excellence, and yield to

God's absolute power and control; one has to relinquish completely the inclination to remain in control. In fact, the sovereignty of God is so encompassing that most of us walk past it, or stumble and fall over it, without realizing.

Are you still there? Good. The purpose of this book is not just to make a *theological statement* about who God is. It is also to share how I began my journey of coming to know the power of God's dominion; it is to encourage you to trust God fully, no matter what circumstances or problems you may experience in life. My desire is that as you read the account of my illness, you will not only see that life is as a mist that may appear for a little while and then vanish, but you will also understand that despite life's brevity, God loves us and has a plan and a purpose for our lives.

You will see how my nothingness survived only *because of* God's sovereignty. From the onset of my illness until my recovery, God's character, importance, excellence, absolute power, and control made themselves evident to me and my family. Time and time again, our family witnessed divine intervention on our behalf, and saw how God used His men and women servants to aid Him in His work. As you journey with us, I trust that you will be awed by the panoramic view of God's power and see how our utter dependence on Him ushered in a depth of relationship and trust that we had not known before. Regardless of our stations in life, I believe each of us will experience a "known encounter" with the Sovereign God. I write this book out of my encounter. It is my prayer that when you are confronted with your struggle, you will come to know and recognize God in a greater way.

Come—watch with me.

Prologue
Another Humdrum Day

———o·⊷✠⊶o———

riday, March 20, 1998 - 7:00 am Buzz-buzz. Buzz-buzz. My alarm clock was reminding me, once again, to wake up and get moving. As I turned the alarm off, I began my day as I always did: on my knees, beside my bed. *Dear God, I thank You for allowing me to see a new day ... Thank You for health, soundness of mind ... Thanks so much for my family ... Thank you so much for Your love ... Let my life bring glory to You this day. In Jesus' name I pray, Amen.* I showered, got dressed, ate breakfast, and rushed off to work.

As a school nurse with the New York City Board of Education, I provided health service and care to students who were mentally, developmentally, and physically challenged. The school day was remarkably uneventful: continual assessment and monitoring of the students, administration of medications and treatments, talking with staff and parents, and providing comfort to the students. This included lots of hugs, rubbing little heads, and wiping teary eyes.

At the end of a hectic day, I was more than ready to leave work. I can remember it being a sunny and pleasant day. I jumped in our BMW and cracked open the window as I headed to pick up my husband, Jerry, in Brooklyn. The signs of spring were bursting forth and my senses were heightened as I began driving. The birds had begun their seasonal melody and the flower buds were in full array, displaying their newly formed color scheme. The smell of freshly cut grass filled the air as I made my way to the outskirts of Cambria Heights. I rolled the window down even further so I could enjoy the crisp breeze. As I approached the north entrance ramp to the Cross Island Parkway, I was pleasantly surprised to see that there was hardly any traffic. But I knew that, sooner or later, I would have to compete with relentless, crazy drivers and potholes, as was always the case in New York. Still, I was ecstatic to be ahead of the rush hour jam. Anticipating the hustle and bustle of Atlantic Avenue, I began to prepare myself, mentally, for the next phase of my journey.

The radio was tuned to a gospel station and I was singing along with one of my favorite artists. Before I knew it, I had reached the extension connecting Queens to Brooklyn. The traffic began to intensify, somewhat, with school buses and commuters jockeying for limited space as we sped down the three-lane "racetrack." Just ahead, I noticed a sudden influx of foot traffic. "The Avenue" was packed with excited school kids escorted by book-bag-toting parents. Mixed in were droves of teenagers mingling in their latest styles. As I waited at the light, I marveled as crossing guards tried their best to do their thankless job amidst the symphony of movement.

It seemed as if there was an "unannounced" street festival and I didn't get the memo. The pizza shops, bodegas, and other eateries overflowed with welcome activities. Music blared from sidewalk speakers which seemed to spur on the "festival." This was just another day on Atlantic Avenue. Though it was a far cry from the more laid-back community where we lived, I always appreciated the change of scenery and the accompanying excitement.

As I continued on Atlantic, I glanced at the clock and realized I was ahead of my scheduled arrival time to pick up Jerry. I decided to change pace and cruise in the extreme right lane so I could take in all the sights and sounds. Despite the dilapidated buildings that were common on almost every overcrowded block, there was something appealing about the architecture of the Clinton Heights area. Those brownstones seemed to tell the story of the people who lived there. They spoke of success and the struggle to survive. The streets were tree lined and the front lawns, though small, were always neatly manicured. I suppose I was distracted by the views because before I knew it, I was making my final right onto Cumberland Street.

Since Jerry had taken public transportation that morning, I pulled into the company's parking lot and parked in his reserved spot. I walked across the street to the security booth and exchanged "hellos" with the guard, who always seemed delighted to see me. I guess that was because I didn't visit Jerry's job often, or maybe he just liked me. The guard called upstairs to let "Mr. Verde" know that I had arrived and I went back to the car to catch a catnap while I waited. It seemed I had just closed my eyes when I heard a light tap on the window. As I opened my eyes, I couldn't tell if the sun was reflecting off of Jerry's easy smile or his bronze, semi-balding head. It was "dress-down Friday," and he was looking quite dapper in his plaid button-down shirt, jeans, and sneakers. In that instant, my heart fluttered when I saw the way he had his sport jacket draped over his shoulder. It reminded me of our younger days when we were enamored simply by each other's presence. I loved it when he looked at me with that certain twinkle in his eyes, and I could hardly wait to kiss those scrumptious lips.

Jerry and I were nineteen and eighteen when we first met. Fresh out of high school, we had migrated to "The Big Apple" from North and South Carolina, respectively. Our paths initially intersected in 1965, while we were attending the same church, Bethel Gospel Tabernacle. We sang in the "Youth for Christ" choir and were actively engaged in the youth department and the church's bible school. Although we didn't necessarily hang in the same circles, we fellowshipped and were "friendly" due to our common activities.

Jerry tells me that he was first smitten when he heard my "melodic" voice while our choir was recording its first album in the summer of '68. I was singing the lead to "We're Gonna Make It" and he knew then that he *had* to get to know the person behind that voice better. At the time, Jerry had just returned from a military tour of duty in Vietnam.

Although I had always admired his spirituality, upon his return from Vietnam, I noticed he had gained weight and his body had filled out. I especially noticed that his arm muscles were bulky and pronounced. Frankly, the brother was looking good.

I can still remember, so vividly, one Sunday afternoon in July 1968 when our choir participated in an outdoor crusade/songfest in St. Albans Park. After the event was over, I climbed aboard our church's yellow-bird bus and asked, "Who's inviting me to dinner today?" You see, back then it was not unusual to extend a self-invitation to a friend's house. And from way in the back of the bus, I heard a muffled response, "I will." I was extremely surprised, to say the least, that the "I will" came from Jerry. After working full-time and attending college part-time in the evenings, a good home-cooked meal sounded terribly inviting. I graciously accepted the invitation and we decided to walk the short distance to Jerry's house instead of riding the bus. Jerry shared an apartment with his sister, Geraldine, and I assumed that she had already prepared dinner. But once we arrived at their home, Jerry rolled up his sleeves and began his culinary show. I watched as he moved around the kitchen with such ease: chopping, seasoning, and stirring. Before long, the aroma caused my mouth to water and I could barely wait to eat. When dinner was almost finished, I offered to set the table. We blessed the food and dug in. He had made the most delicious stuffed pork chops. Oh my, was I impressed! Every morsel was scrumptious. My belly was full and Jerry's foot was in the "door of my heart."

Our first date was the following Sunday after church. Jerry took me to a very chic local restaurant called Constantine. It was during dinner that I officially became the second member of "The Smitten Team." And it didn't take long before we both knew that we were in love and wanted to be married. On one frigidly cold winter night in February 1969, Jerry slipped a beautiful pear-shaped diamond engagement ring on my finger and we sealed that special moment with a kiss under the big flood light in front of Kiely Hall on the Queens College campus. We were married on October 4, 1969. And within five years, we were the proud parents of an incredible son, Arnold, and a splendiferous daughter, Tracey.

By March 1998, we had seen our children through college and they were settled and living on their own. Finally, Jerry and I were ready to focus on the ministerial call that we knew God had placed on our lives. During our marriage, we had become mentors to younger couples in our church and within our community. These couples had observed our marriage and family relationships and often came to us for encouragement. Not only did we offer advice to a plethora of couples, but God graced our family to be a template for our children's friends as well. Our home was like Time Square, a place where Arnold and Tracey's friends gathered. Their parents knew that their children would be safe, happy, well cared for, and especially well fed. Jerry has filled many a hungry belly with his "world famous pancake breakfast." As a result of these combined life experiences, we knew that God would ultimately birth in us a family life ministry.

We were excited about fulfilling the vision God had given us to become ministers, so we enrolled in a Master of Divinity degree program at a seminary in New York City for the fall semester. To prepare ourselves, we knew we needed a better understanding of our "alien" computer. We were scheduled to begin a computer course that evening in Manhattan (in the Wall Street area) to help us keep up with technology and not become "fuddy-duddies."

When we arrived at the course site, the program coordinator informed us that the class was overbooked. She apologized and rescheduled us for the following Friday. We were slightly disappointed, but we were determined to make the best of the evening.

Jerry and I left the building hand in hand, full of chitchat and reminiscing as we pointed out several familiar buildings. We had strolled along those same streets together many years before, making plans for our wedding and our new life together. During our courtship, we had both held jobs in the banking industry and worked in that area. We would long for the lunch hours we spent together dreaming about our future. After we reached our car and left the parking lot, I had this sudden desire to see the old building where I worked my first full-time job after coming to New York from South Carolina. I asked Jerry if he knew how to get to Church Street, and after a few "guesstimate" turns, we wound up on the street right across from the building.

Caught up in the spirit of reminiscing, I suggested that we drive through Chinatown, where we had many fun dates eating and window shopping for my engagement ring during our courtship. Once we reached Chinatown, we giggled and carried on like teenagers. It was a far cry from the Canal Street we knew, but being there brought back such fond memories. It was fun! Finally, we found our way to the Brooklyn-Queens Expressway for our drive home and decided to pick up dinner on the way. We arrived home at about 9:00 pm and sat for a while in the breakfast nook, eating and catching up on the day's events.

In preparation for my "rest and relaxation" after the long work week, I ran a warm bubble bath and gathered a few books to read. Jerry showered, put on his favorite red flannel pajamas, and retreated to our family room in the basement for his own "R&R." After I finished my bath and was dressed for bed, I called my friend, Gloria, to catch up on some "sistah-girl" talk. Both our schedules were so hectic that we didn't get a chance to chat as often as we would have liked. I was finally able to reach her at about 11:15 pm.

Jerry's R&R would generally last well into the wee hours of Saturday morning, so I decided to take advantage of this bit of free time. Most often, I didn't even know when he came to bed. I suspect he and the television would alternate watching each other. But on this particular Friday night, Jerry came up to bed at 11:30 and lay on my side of the bed. I was lying on his side of the bed where I continued, briefly, in conversation with Gloria. When I ended my conversation, Jerry was asleep—or so I thought. Not wanting to disturb his comfortable sleeping position, I touched him lightly on his shoulder and asked him to switch pillows with me; my pillow was softer than his. Instead, Jerry got up and walked around the bed to his side, and I slid over to my side. It was such a simple and seemingly mundane action. I can still see Jerry's image at the foot of our bed.

Then my picture went blank.

Unbeknownst to me, I was experiencing a succession of four Grand Mal seizures, which hit me one after the other. The graphic above is an attempt to capture the chaos that was taking place in my body during the seizures.

Chapter One
The Eyewitness Account

M uch of the immediate events surrounding my "near-death" experience on March 21, 1998 are either silent or very vague in my memory. But there was an eyewitness to the whole account: my husband, Jerry. He has assured me how blessed I am that God sheltered my memory from the trauma that my body endured during the critical time of my emergency treatment.

As a result of a multitude of experiences, I've come to embrace a wonderful yiddish word, *bashert*, which means a destined love or soul mate. I believe this word best describes Jerry. Before I was formed in my mother's womb, God knew that on March 21 I would need a "destined love" that could see, hear, and speak for me when I was unable to do any of those things for myself. Jerry did just that. He is my bashert.

~

This explains why a man leaves his father and mother and is joined to his wife in such a way that the two become one person.

Genesis 2:24 (TLB)

~

One of the beautiful things about our marriage is that sometimes I feel as if I inhale the essence or the spirit that Jerry exhales. So often, I am hard-pressed to delineate where I stop and where he begins.

Jerry echoes this thought. Although we are temperamentally suited for each other, we have not lost an appreciation for the uniqueness of our individuality. For example, Jerry is somewhat bubbly and I am rather reserved. The positive to both is that Jerry's bubbly personality keeps us with lots of friends and my demure *don't try it* attitude keeps "the crazies" at bay. We celebrate the gift and strength of our unity.

Jerry and I have a good "seesaw" rhythm in our marriage. In any of our life situations, one of us gets to be up while the other is in the down position. As such, when I am in the up position, I've learned to enjoy the air and the exhilaration it brings because it is inevitable that my next position will be down. But the paradox of "our ride" is that even when I'm in the down position, I'm also in the up position because Jerry is there. After all, we are one flesh. We try not to resist this movement. We simply relax, allowing the natural cadence of our marriage to unfold so that we can, equally, enjoy the ride. This explains why a man leaves his father and mother and is joined to his wife in such a way that the two become one person.

In the early morning hours of March 21, Jerry sprang into action when my picture was blank, when there was an interruption in my awareness of being, and I lost the ability to make decisions for myself. He did *for* me then what he had done **with** me during our twenty-nine years of marriage; he changed "the two become one flesh" from the *Logos* (written) Word of God to the *Rhema* (living) Word of God.

As sight is to my eyes, sound to my ears, taste to my tongue, feel to my touch, and love to my heart, so is Jerry to my life. Let's listen in on Jerry's story as he shares more about the miracle that took place on March 21.

Jerry's Story

On this particular Friday evening, my week's-end R&R, as Agnes likes to call it, consisted of watching a fascinating documentary entitled *The Taking of Hill 8088*. This story was about how the American troops battled to take Hill 8088 in the republic of South Vietnam, during the Vietnam War. As a medic in Vietnam, I was quite intrigued by the program, and watched it to its riveting conclusion at 11:00 pm. After taking in the local news, I left the family room to go upstairs. I wanted to share my excitement with Agnes about the documentary's visualization of how the American troops conquered "the Hill."

When I reached our bedroom, she was talking on the phone, so I decided to lie down on her side of the bed. At around 11:45 pm, when she finished her call, Agnes asked me to switch pillows with her. Though I was almost in "la-la" land, I told her I would come around to my side of the bed so she could just slide over. I reached my side of the bed, turned off the light, knelt, prayed, and climbed into bed.

Once I got comfortable, I asked, "Agnes, did you see that documentary on Vietnam?" She didn't respond. Actually, she seemed to snicker and the bed shook slightly. Puzzled that she would snicker at that question, I repeated, "Did you see that documentary on Vietnam?!" Still there was no response. *Why is she not answering my question?* I thought. Then I heard Agnes take a deep, sighing breath. Immediately, a combination of panic and instinct set in. At that moment, I was not sure why she did not respond, but I knew with every fiber of my being that something was terribly wrong.

By the time I reached for the light and turned to look at Agnes's face, her eyes had rolled upward in her head and she was in a fixed stare. I shouted her name several times, "Agnes! Agnes! Agnes!" but she did not respond. Then I cried out, "Jesus! Jesus! Jesus!" Agnes's head then began to move rapidly from side to side. After a few seconds, the movement stopped and then began again. I couldn't wrap my brain around what was happening. *How could this be? She was just talking on the phone!* She hadn't complained that anything was wrong and I didn't notice any unusual behavior in the hours leading up to that moment.

My mind was racing—trying to understand, trying to think back, trying to remember things, trying ... Just then, her head began to rapidly thrust from side to side in a jagged repetition. With violent spasms, her entire body seemed to be in a fight with itself as white foam oozed from her mouth. Desperately, I called her name again, "Agnes! Agnes!" No response. That's when I realized she was probably having seizures. I had a flashback! I remembered seeing men having seizures when I was in the war. Little did I know, the biggest battle of our lives was about to begin.

I turned her head to the side and called 911. The operator answered and immediately began rambling off questions about the emergency at hand. Somehow, I managed to explain what was happening and begged her to send an ambulance immediately. I remember changing quickly from my pajama bottom into a pair of pants. Miraculously, in less than five minutes I saw the reflection of flashing lights against our bedroom walls. When I looked out of the window, I was amazed to see an EMS Unit stopping in front of our house. I ran downstairs to let them in and escorted them upstairs.

When the EMS technicians looked at Agnes, I could tell by the looks on their faces that something was severely wrong. Agnes was still not responding. They put an oxygen mask over her face, and after quickly assessing her responsiveness to stimuli, placed her in a portable chair to carry her down to the ambulance. When they placed Agnes in the chair, her body stretched out completely and became as stiff as a board. They waited for her body to relax and continued down the stairs. During the transport, I heard the male EMS tech on his headset requesting that a second EMS unit be sent over, *stat!* He must have known that they were not equipped to handle the severity of this emergency. Once they placed Agnes in the ambulance, they moved about rapidly, working on her. I didn't know exactly what they were doing, but they were focused on communicating with each other and whoever was on the other end of the headset.

Then I could hear the blaring siren of the second EMS unit, which came and parked behind the first. Two techs from the second unit jumped out of the cab and entered the first, each carrying large metal cases. I watched as the four of them worked vigorously on Agnes, inserting an IV line and injecting her with medication. Still, she was not responding. Finally, they asked me to step back as they closed the door.

After about ten long minutes, one of the EMS techs informed me that Agnes had to be taken to the hospital. I requested that she be taken to the hospital where she had previously worked, but was told that the distance was too great given the severity of her illness. I was given the choice of two closer hospitals—one a large medical center and the other a small community hospital. Ordinarily, the large medical center would have been my choice. But as I reflect, I know now that it was divine intervention that made me choose the latter.

The ambulance left for the hospital at approximately 12:30 am. I hurried upstairs, finished dressing, and rushed to the car. As I looked at the dashboard, of all the times, I was low on gas! I made a quick stop and got just enough gas to make it to the hospital.

Upon my arrival, I identified myself to the emergency-room nurse and asked, "Where is my wife, Agnes Greene?" She directed me to cubicle one. When I reached the cubicle, I saw a woman there but I did not know her. This woman's face and body were so grossly distorted and disfigured that I was certain the nurse had made a mistake. So I went back to the nurse, asking again, "Where is my wife, Agnes Greene?" Much to my chagrin, she directed me back to cubicle one.

On my way back, I recognized the four EMS techs that had responded to my 911 call. They were scurrying to assist the ER staff with the "woman in cubicle one," the one I didn't recognize. It was then that I was struck with the reality that this was, indeed, my darling wife. Agnes was wearing an oxygen mask and her face was swollen to about one and a half times its normal size. She lay completely motionless and her closed eyes protruded like frogs. Her lips were grossly engorged, as if they had been injected with collagen. The ER staff and EMS personnel continued to move around me, attending to Agnes. I became overwhelmed, questioning, *God, how could all of this happen in just an hour?*

Then a man dressed in a green outfit brought in some sort of machine and I was asked to step out. They pulled the curtain, separating me and my wife. At that moment, I felt as if I was in a time warp; as if a veil had been lowered. I could see and touch her but I felt an overwhelming sense of helplessness and hopelessness. None of this made any sense. Frantic thoughts kept resurfacing. *How can this be? Agnes was fine … and now this?* I felt so confused. A short while later, a woman approached me and identified herself as the emergency room head nurse. She began asking me questions. "Do you have any children?" I responded, "Yes, a son and a daughter."

"What is your religious persuasion?"

I answered, "Protestant."

Then she said the words no one ever wants to hear: "Call your children. Call your minister. Tell them to come as quickly as possible. As of a few minutes ago, the doctor has listed your wife as comatose. There's nothing else we can do."

When I heard the word *comatose* I felt as if everything inside of me fell down to the floor, as if I'd dropped a robe from my body. I began to sob, uncontrollably.

I could hear myself asking, "God, what am I going to do without Agnes?" A dam of tears burst forth and I continued sobbing for what seemed like an eternity. Then the Holy Spirit whispered, "Stop crying. There are things I need you to do."

I stepped outside of the hospital to make some calls on my cell phone. First, I called my sister, Geraldine. As soon as she answered the phone, I began sobbing again. Even through my gasps, Geral recognized my voice. "Jerry, what's the matter?"

I told her, "Agnes is gone."

She responded, "Gone where?"

I said, "She is in a coma and it doesn't look good."

Geral was shocked as I recounted the events of the past hour. "Where are you?" she asked me. I told her the name of the hospital. "Is there anybody with you?"

"No! No! Nobody's here but me and Agnes," I told her between sobs. She said she would call around and have someone come to be with me. She prayed with me and hung up.

Then I called our family doctor and left a message on his answering machine, asking him to return my call. Shortly afterward, he called me back. When I told him what happened, he was in total disbelief. He literally broke down in tears. It was no wonder—Agnes and I had had our annual physical at his office the day before. We'd had no complaints or concerns and had been given a clean bill of health. After he gathered himself, he told me that he did not have admitting privileges at the hospital where we were but he knew a "journeyman" (fellow physician) who was on staff there. He asked my permission to have this doctor cover Agnes and assured me that he would be kept abreast daily. I agreed.

After Jerry's call went out to his sister, Geraldine, she contacted a friend of our family, Rosie Parris, who is one of God's generals in the faith. She began to enlist warriors for the battle at hand. —AG

Rosie Sheard Parris
The Call

As I sat writing cards, assisting with a Women's Auxiliary request from my church, the telephone rang. "Hello?"

The voice on the other end was Geraldine and she immediately responded, "Agnes is critically ill—Pray!"

I sat for a minute, still writing. I was stunned, to say the least! Wanting to respect their privacy, I thought, *I wonder if Jerry wants me to tell anyone?* Suddenly, I said, "Jerry is with Agnes! He probably can't think beyond the immediate." So, I grabbed my telephone book, thinking … thinking … thinking, *who should I call?*

I called those that I knew loved to pray, as well as very close friends of mine and Jerry and Agnes. As each call was answered, I said, "Agnes is critically ill!" Each would ask, "What's the matter?" I responded, "Pray!"

and I hung up. I called the next person: "Pray!" Click. And the next: "Pray!" Click. The urgent request for prayer was repeated until I had called about forty praying people. Not knowing who else to call, I said, "Dear Jesus, who else should I call?" Immediately, I was reminded of the Prayer Ministry of one of our church deacons. "O Dear Jesus. He loves to pray!" And I called Deacon Frank. He answered the phone as if he was expecting the call. He responded to my appeal with, "I am praying right now."

My next call was to our children. As I began dialing the numbers, I noticed it had begun to drizzle. For some reason, the rain was so comforting to me. It felt cleansing. It helped to purge some of the pain I was feeling.

When I reached the car, I called Tracey. Her phone rang … and rang … and rang. But she did not answer. Then I called Arnold. When he answered the phone, without much forethought, I blurted out, "Your mother took sick and she might be gone!" Arnold asked, "Gone where?" And I told him, "Gone to heaven!"

"Daddy! Daddy! Daddy! What happened to Mommy?" Arnold screamed.

I told him what happened and remembered myself saying, "She is listed as comatose. It doesn't look good Arnold! It doesn't look good!" Then we both began crying, each trying to console the other. "I've been trying to reach Tracey but she is not answering her phone," I told Arnold. "Try to reach her and I'll call you back as soon as I find out more." I hung up with Arnold and returned to the emergency room.

As I sat in the waiting area for what seemed like an eternity, suddenly a voice came over the intercom: "Jerry Greene, Jerry Greene. Please return to the treatment area." The only thought that came to my mind was that they would tell me that my wife had died. *And I was not ready to hear that!* My mind reverted back to when they had pulled the curtain around the cubicle where Agnes's lifeless-looking body lay, and I was asked to step outside.

When I got up from my seat, my legs felt like rubber, my head was pounding and I felt as if I wanted to vomit. I could feel the warm tears flowing from my eyes. And no matter how hard I tried, I could not stop them. As I made my way through the automatic doors leading to the treatment area, I heard someone calling my name, "Jerry! Jerry!" When I turned toward the voice, my nephew, Terry, and my cousin, Bettye were running toward me. Unbeknownst to me, my sister had contacted them and asked them to come be with me. What divine timing! They began asking questions about Agnes, but I didn't have time to explain anything. I knew I needed to get to the treatment area, but I was so grateful that they were there. I linked arms with them, Terry on one side and Bettye on the other, and asked them both to go in with me. I knew I would need their support for the news that I *thought* I was about to receive. Only God could have orchestrated them to arrive at precisely the right moment, in precisely the right place.

At that moment, I could feel the battle intensifying between my mind and my spirit—I felt like David did in many of the Psalms he wrote in the bible. My mind screamed: *What am I going to do without Agnes?* My spirit declared: *God, You are my refuge and my strength!* My mind asked: *What if she doesn't pull through?* My spirit announced: *God, You are my very present help in trouble!* Mind: *How will I make it without Agnes?* Spirit: *God, I trust You with my whole heart!* Admittedly, the thought that was prevalent and kept replaying in my mind was: *What am I going to do without Agnes?*

As we approached the treatment area, the head nurse was waiting and asked me to sit down at a desk. She informed me that Agnes was still in a comatose state and still not responsive. I was braced for the worst! To my astonishment, she explained that the medical staff was cautiously optimistic regarding Agnes's condition. She further explained that a person in a comatose state is thought to still hear what is going on in their environment. As such, I was encouraged to talk to Agnes, and she tried to prepare me for what I would see when I returned to cubicle one.

When Terry, Bettye, and I reached the cubicle, there lay Agnes's motionless body. A small tube was coming from her nose and a larger one protruded from her mouth; each tube was connected to a machine. There were multiple IV lines and other tubes attached to various parts of her body. I thought, *My God! How can her body tolerate all of this prodding?* Terry found it hard to believe that this was really Agnes. Her face appeared more horrific than before. Her body seemed even more contorted than it was just a few hours before. Terry kept walking around the bed, shaking his head in disbelief, saying over and over, "This is not Agnes! This is not Agnes!"

As the nurse had encouraged me, I began to rub her hand as I whispered in her ear, "Baby, I'm here and Terry and Bettye are with me." I wanted her to feel my breath in her ear. I kept telling Agnes how much I loved her and how much our family needed her. I told her I had contacted Arnold and that he and Tracey were on their way to see her.

In the background, it seemed as if the telephones in the treatment area were ringing off the hook. Many of our friends were calling to inquire about Agnes's condition. The calls were so frequent that one of the emergency room's telephone lines was specifically designated for our family. I asked Terry to go and talk to the callers. Bettye was on the other side of Agnes's bed, holding and rubbing her hand. I was so thankful to God that she was there, because she had extensive experience working in a hospital. I tried to explain to Agnes all that the staff was doing for her and continued to tell her how much I loved and needed her.

As I spoke, one of the machines she was attached to started to beep and kept beeping repeatedly. I looked at Bettye. She had this strange look on her face, and she mouthed the words, "She has no pulse! She has no pulse!" I tried to ignore what she was mouthing and kept talking to Agnes, all the while pleading, "God! Don't let Agnes die! Don't let Agnes die!" Several nurses and doctors came rushing to the bedside and, again, asked us to step out of the treatment area.

After what seemed like an eternity, Bettye and I were allowed to go back into the room. I kept talking to Agnes as the doctors and nurses administered care. Again, the respirator started beeping repeatedly. Although I didn't know what she meant at the time, I remember Bettye asking the doctor, rather emphatically, "Is she bucking the respirator?" The doctor came and made some adjustments to the machine. Shortly afterward, Agnes began flailing her arms. The doctor decided that Agnes's arms had to be restrained to prevent her from pulling out the tubes or further injuring herself. Initially, they restrained her with gauze-like arm restraints, but her resistance became so violent that she snapped them like the Incredible Hulk! They explained that they needed to crisscross her restraints underneath the bed for better reinforcement. Although I understood that type of restraint was necessary for her safety, I felt as if I had failed Agnes in a sense. The respirator began beeping again, repeatedly, and Bettye asked again, "Isn't she bucking the respirator?" A short while later, the ER attending doctor entered the cubicle and determined that she was, indeed, attempting to breathe on her own. Sometime later, he ordered that she be disconnected. I've learned, subsequently, that this was done to see if she could breathe independent of the respirator. After it was determined that she could, the large tube in her mouth was also removed.

I learned later, in layman's terms, that the settings on a respirator are synchronized to mimic the patient's breathing pattern. If the respirator's "inhalation and exhalation" pattern gets out of sync with the patient's breathing pattern, the respirator has the capacity to overwhelm or "suffocate" the patient if the patient should attempt to breath on her own.

Even though we began to observe glimpses of hope, it was obvious Agnes was still in such a struggle. It seemed as if her body was in total resistance to what was happening to her. Because she was so restless, medication to sedate her was ordered. After the medication was given, she would calm down for a while, but then the struggle would ensue again.

~

It seemed as if God separated the part of me that loved Agnes so much, that I could hardly stand to see her in such a battle from the part of me that had to help save her life.

~

During this period, I felt as if God sedated me, also. I actually felt numb. It seemed as if God separated the part of me that loved Agnes so much, that I could hardly stand to see her in such a battle from the part of me that had to help save her life. I had to give voice to Agnes's fight to live. If I had operated only in the "love portion" of our relationship, I would have been paralyzed and ineffective.

As I watched and prayed, I thought about this great woman I had married twenty-eight years before. Agnes was a woman of tremendous strength, determination, and faith. She had so much to live for: our new granddaughter, GiGi, was just ten days old. We had plans for ministry, and there were other personal projects she wanted to complete. In the spirit realm, I knew she was safe with God, suspended somewhere between time and eternity. And though I was physically in the natural realm, I knew I had to enact spiritual warfare on her behalf because I didn't believe her purpose on earth was finished. And so I prayed and talked, prayed and talked, prayed some more and talked even more.

After a few hours had passed, I asked Agnes a question. "Baby, do you want them to take the tube out of your nose? If so, just squeeze my hand." To my total delight, she squeezed my hand. I told the nurse what had taken place and asked if the remaining tube could be removed from her nose. The nurse said she would inform the doctor of my request. A short while later, I asked the staff to remove her arm restraints as well. Surprisingly, they complied, though the tube in her nose was still in place. Once the restraints were off, Agnes appeared to be resting more comfortably and seemed less agitated. But my Agnes does not quit until she gets what she is due! Shortly thereafter, she reached up with an amazing exactness and pulled the tube right out of her nose! I told the nurse what had happened. She assessed Agnes to determine if any trauma was done. Again, the nurse said that she would make the doctor aware. In her unconscious state, Agnes still had a resolve to live! I rejoiced in the fact that she was fighting so hard to live.

Not long after she pulled the tube out of her nose, Agnes suddenly sat up in the bed, opened her eyes, and said these four precious words: "I … need … to … pee!" Those words were like music to my ears! I felt as if I was instantly on "cloud nine." I shot back, "*Pee … baby … pee!*" She then laid her head back on her pillow and drifted back to sleep. Although she continued in and out of consciousness, I knew that moment that Agnes would be coming back to us!

Around 11:30 on the morning of March 21, the ER staff informed me that Agnes would not be going to the Intensive Care Unit, as was previously planned. Instead, she would be admitted to a regular room on a medical floor by noon. Agnes was still resting and drifting in and out of sleep due to the medication. As she was being transported from the emergency room to the floor, it suddenly dawned on me that I had been a firsthand witness to God's miracles during the past twelve hours.

When we arrived at the nurses' station on the receiving floor, I said to Agnes, "I love you so much." She looked back at me with those great big beautiful eyes and said, "Give me a big hug!" What a pleasure it was to hug her again—and I added a kiss, too. There was not a dry eye at the nurses' station. It was then that God allowed me to transition from advocate and provider back to being her lover.

After the staff got Agnes settled in bed, she fell off to sleep, quickly. Terry had to leave the hospital to check in at home. Bettye stayed in the room with Agnes, and I decided to go downstairs to get a bite to eat. As I was about to bite into my bacon and egg sandwich, I saw Arnold and Tracey entering the lobby. I completely lost my appetite as I jumped up to greet them. When I reached them, we hugged and kissed and for the moment I felt a tremendous sense of peace. They were a welcome and beautiful sight for my sore eyes.

As we left the lobby on our way to Agnes's room, I shared with them the events of the night. I wanted to prepare them for the condition in which they would find their mother. They were asking a lot of questions about the night's events and wanted to know the long-term prognosis. God knew exactly what I needed after the long, lonely night. After they were sure that Agnes was stable, their next question was, "Daddy, how are you doing? How are you feeling?" I didn't really have an answer, but before I could try to respond, they both grabbed and hugged me. It was strong, yet so tender. And did I need that!

Later that afternoon, the "journeyman" that was attending Agnes came to introduce himself. He was a soft-spoken and kind man. His demeanor was very soothing. He said that he would be there for us and he assured me that he would keep our family doctor informed of every aspect of Agnes's care. His news, however, was not all good. He informed us the CAT scan showed that there was possibly a mass on Agnes's brain. He said he would order an MRI and a neurologist would come to evaluate further. Though Agnes was heavily sedated, and at times would fall asleep in the middle of her sentence, when she awoke, she was alert and able to converse coherently.

The next day was Sunday. And oh what a Sabbath! Agnes was pretty upbeat and chatty with the steady stream of family and friends who came from near and far to visit. If the number of visitors was any indication of how much she was loved, she would certainly not have a concern in the world. I was heartened to see that she interacted with her guests as if the events of the past two days had never happened. Even more, I was ever so grateful to God for sparing her the horrible remembrance of the previous days' trauma.

On Monday, March 23, Agnes had the MRI done, which confirmed a mass the size of a lemon. She was transferred to North Shore Medical Center on Tuesday, March 24, where surgery would be done to remove the tumor. Agnes repeatedly expressed that she did not want to have surgery. But after much prayer and our show of support, she conceded that if it was necessary, she would do it. Although it was difficult for me to even think of her going through any more trauma I assured her that whatever decision she made, I would support her wholeheartedly.

We met with the operating surgeon and his team. We were told that the mass was located in a "good spot," the silent part of her brain. What this meant was that, barring any complications, there should be no adverse effect on Agnes's vision, speech, or mobility. The doctor cautioned us that there are risks associated with any surgical invasion of the body. He told us that Agnes's procedure would be done using "stereo-taxic" markings on her scalp. These markings would pinpoint the precise location of the tumor, thereby causing the least amount of damage to healthy tissues surrounding the tumor site. The operating surgeon and his team were pioneers in this type of procedure. It was the sovereign act of God that connected us to this world-renowned neurosurgical team through the neurologist at the "small hospital." We recognize God as our maker so we trusted God to direct the hands of these "vessels" to safely and successfully complete the surgery.

I am told that after Rosie's "Call to Prayer" went out, the saints began bombarding Heaven on our behalf. The power of prayer can be likened to an intercontinental guided missile. It has the capacity to be fired from a location in one continent and hit its target in another continent. Christians were praying for us nationwide, even in Europe. And for your obedience and commitment to the welfare of the body of Christ, we are eternally grateful. You kept our cause before God and He honored His Word!

Chapter Two
From The Heart of a Child

———o·❦·o———

Teach a child how he [she] should live, and
he [she] will remember it all his [her] life
Proverbs 22:6 (Good News Bible)

*J*erry and I are the proud parents of three wonderful children, two
*of whom we were gifted through the miracle of birth: Arnold and
Tracey. And one of whom we were gifted through the miracle of love:
Doneisha (Arnold's wife). The above scripture was the principle that guided
us as we raised our children. Though Arnold and Tracey are adults now,
we continue to believe and relax in its promise.*

*Please allow me an encouraging moment: from my heart to the hearts
of other parents. The first part of this biblical quote, "Teach a child how
he [she] should live …," is our parental obligation. As our children were
entering adulthood and began to experiment with different life situations,
sometimes without our approval, we were, at times, disturbed and became
distracted. But had we embraced the promise that God gives to us, as
parents, in the second part of this scripture, "and he [she] will remember it
all his [her] life," this would not have been our experience.*

*We would do well to always be cognizant of the fact that God has so
much more invested in our children than we have. We are merely vessels
that usher our children into this space called earth and this motion called*

time. When we have fulfilled our parental obligation to teach (train) our children, this, then, becomes their "journey." It is then we must trust God to remind our children of the principles we've given them. This teaching/ training will allow them to navigate through life.

In a letter I wrote to Arnold, Tracey, and Doneisha while recovering from the surgery, I shared how "God has used each of you as a source of inspiration and encouragement to me during this most difficult time. I know that God took this experience and has caused you to be stronger in your faith in God, as my faith has also been made stronger." The writing of this book is not only a testimony to the miracle that God worked in my life, but it will attest, also, to how God used this miracle to affect the lives of our family and many others.

Very often when a family experiences a crisis, not everyone is given the chance to express or choose to express how he or she is affected. As a result, feelings and emotions are suppressed, and quite often these suppressed feelings and emotions may resurface, expressed in distorted behaviors. I felt that it was imperative to our emotional health that our children participate in this writing. Their love and support were critical components of my healing.

I've asked Arnold, Tracey, and Doneisha to share how they were affected by this crisis. Listen in on them as they share from their hearts. —AG

Arnold's Heart

Daddy's first baby, Gianni Alaina Greene, was in her white bassinet next to me and my wife Doneisha. She was so beautiful. I couldn't keep my eyes off of her. I wanted to constantly hug and kiss her, but it was two in the morning and she had succumbed to the "sleep monster." Daddy and Mommy needed some rest, too.

We were cramped in the guest bedroom at my in-laws', Mrs. Ginny and Mr. Roland, and I was thinking how much I'd love to be home in my own bed. By the same token, I was extremely grateful that Mrs. Ginny wanted her two "little girls" near her so she could assist Doneisha, who was recovering from a caesarean section.

Then there was a knock on the door. Mama Ginny said, "Lee (my nickname), telephone—it's your father." Immediately, my heart started to race. The only news that could come at this time of the morning was bad news. I thought something terrible must have happened to one of my uncles or some other relative, or my father would have waited to call later in the day. Though I awoke out of a deep sleep, I was completely alert by the time Mama Ginny handed me the phone. I awaited the bad news.

The voice I heard was unlike any voice I had ever known before. It was Daddy's voice, but the level of despair in it was unrecognizable to me. He mumbled something like, "Your mother is in a coma," but his words were drowned out by his violent sobs. It was then I realized that something serious had happened, but Daddy was so distraught that he told me he had to call me right back. At that point, I guess my newfound paternal instinct "kicked in." I realized that I had to be strong, and in essence, I needed to be the "surrogate" patriarch of the family. I stood ready to fill that role—or so I thought.

In the few minutes between Daddy's calls, I remember Doneisha asking me what happened when the phone rang. After I explained what I knew at that point, she tried to comfort me. But in that moment, I didn't need comfort. It didn't seem like enough. I focused on the words my mother would always tell me: "God does all things well." I knew this was a time to believe that for whatever reason this situation was happening, it was ordained by God—even though I still didn't clearly understand.

The phone rang again. This time, Daddy was a little more composed and able to explain what had happened. He told me to stay in Maryland until he found out more. I'm sure he was concerned about my driving at that time in the morning. I asked him to keep me informed and to call back, no matter the time. Immediately, I started making plans to pick up Tracey on the way to New York. I put in numerous calls to her, only to hear her wonderful answering machine voice. I left a message, asking her to return my call "ASAP."

Tracey's Heart

"Tomorrow's going to be just another day in the life of Tracey A. Greene." It seemed like it would be the same as any other day. Being the "new-jack" at work definitely had its drawbacks. I got off at 6:30 pm on Friday and was due back again bright and shiny at seven o'clock on Saturday morning. So there was no time to do anything else but eat, shower, wind down, watch a little TV and get some shut-eye. But before I went to bed, there was one last thing I needed to do, call and say "hi" to Ma.

The phone rang, and she answered. My parents had finally caught up with technology and had gotten rid of the rotary-dial phone. You couldn't tell them anything then. And since they discovered the call-waiting feature, they could hardly keep their phone line free! Ma said she was on the phone with Miss Gloria and would call me back. And so I waited and waited, but no callback. Apparently, I waited for a long while because when I woke up, the TV was watching me, and I didn't remember hearing the phone ring. At that point, I didn't want to hear the phone or anything else, for that matter. So I set the alarm clock, turned the volume down on the answering machine, and shut off the ringer on my phone. I reasoned that if anyone called, it wouldn't be that important, right?

Wrong.

It was Saturday morning, March 21 and I woke up twenty minutes late, in a panic. I thought if I washed up quickly and brushed my teeth, I could still make it to work on time. As I grabbed my keys off the nightstand and headed for the door, I noticed the blinking light on the answering machine: *One new message.* I ignored it, jumped in my car, raced downtown, and made it to work in the nick of time.

Once I got settled, I picked up the phone to retrieve my new message. I figured it was one of my friends calling late at night to tell me about some fun they'd had without me. But the voice I heard did not indicate anyone was having fun. It was a familiar voice, but it was filled with a pain that I had never heard before. I knew it was Daddy, but I had never heard him cry like this—a grieving cry.

The intensity of the agony in the words he spoke was deafening. He said, "Tracey?—*sniff, sniff.* This is your father—*sniff, sniff.* Your mother is in the emergency room. She had some seizures tonight and the doctors don't think she's going to make it—*sob.* You need to get here as soon as possible. I asked Arnold to pick you up—*sob.*"

"Call Arnold," he said. *Sniff, sniff.*

I thought, "She's not going to make *what?*" I was hoping we were rehearsing a scene from a horror movie and the director forgot to say, "Cut!" But I knew this was real, and the tears began to flow, and panic started to set in.

The phones I was supposed to be answering were ringing off the hook. I didn't care! All I knew right then was that my mom might be gone and I never got the chance to speak to her last night.

Now I understand much better the old saying, "God knows best." I believe God knew how I would have dealt with this news, alone. Since I missed the call, I missed the emergency room scene. I was spared from having to deal with the immediate and intimate trauma of the night's horrific events, which my father later described. God knew that I wouldn't have been able to handle it and He was right.

Doneisha's Heart

I was up nursing our newborn baby, and my husband was somewhere between awake and asleep. I remember looking down at her and telling her how lucky she was to have two sets of grandparents, an aunt and an uncle, and especially, a mom and dad who were just crazy in love with her. Really, we were in awe. You see, Gianni Alaina Greene was the first grandchild born to both my in-laws, Agnes and Jerry, and to my parents, Ginny and Roland. I can recall my mother's knock at the door. I thought she was just up checking on the baby, but she said the phone was for Lee. Instantly, he jumped up. Now, I know I don't have to tell you that getting a phone call at two in the morning is not usually good news. My mother handed Lee the phone, saying, "It's your father." Instantly, my stomach had butterflies. All I could think was, "What aunt, uncle, or cousin is injured or dead?" I watched Lee as he listened to his father on the phone, all the while trying to read his expressions. The only problem was he had none.

He told his father that he would get in touch with Tracey and he would be leaving after he spoke with her. I knew that the situation had to be grim for Arnold Greene to get on the road at three o'clock in the morning and drive to New York from Maryland. More important, I knew it had to be an emergency if he was willing to leave his almost two-week-old baby girl.

He hung up the phone, looked at me without any emotion or facial expression and said, "My mother has had ..." That's all I can remember him saying, because I pretty much went numb after hearing those first few words. I asked him to repeat himself. "My mother has had some seizures. She is in a coma and they don't think she is going to make it through the night. So I need to go pick up Tracey in Philly and then we're going to meet my father at the hospital." I felt catatonic. I was in complete shock and disbelief. I couldn't even think of anything to say.

We both just started to pack his bags. I felt helpless. I knew I couldn't go to comfort and support Lee and his family, but I was so afraid and upset. I felt as if things were happening around me too fast, yet I was moving in slow motion. I didn't know what to say or how to act toward my own husband. I didn't know *how* to console him. What scared me most was that I couldn't even tell if he wanted or needed to be consoled.

Arnold's Heart

At around seven in the morning, I received the call from Tracey. She was obviously overwhelmed and concerned about the message on her machine. I assured her that as soon as I heard from Daddy, I would come and get her. Daddy and I were in contact throughout the morning. He kept saying that they were still evaluating and trying to stabilize Ma. I was hopeful until another call came.

"Arnold, you need to come now! The doctor said that all immediate family members should come to the hospital as soon as possible. Go get Tracey! Come as soon as you can!" Daddy began to wail. I knew Ma's condition was dire. He sobbed into the phone, "I don't know what I am going to do without Agnes!" And I understood what he meant. You see, in my eyes, they are inseparable. *What is he going to do without Ma?* I thought. I tried to console Daddy as I reminded him of the familiar words I'd heard growing up: "God does all things well!" I don't know if it helped him, but those words surely comforted me.

Doneisha's Heart

When Lee was all packed and about to leave, he gave me a quick kiss and a hug without any emotion whatsoever. He picked up his newborn baby girl- kissing, smelling, and hugging her. He held her for a few minutes, staring into her sleeping face. It was as if he was doing this so he could remember her feel, her scent, and her precious face. He told me he loved us and would call when he arrived in New York. Then, he turned and was gone.

At that moment, my emotions did a 180-degree turn. I went from being scared and upset to feeling angry and cheated. *How can this be happening to us? This is supposed to be the happiest time in our lives. We haven't even had a chance to enjoy our baby, to even have it set in that we are parents!* A part of our joy had been stolen from us. My husband had to stare at and smell and feel his daughter for a few minutes so he could take those token memories with him to last through this difficult time. Gianni hadn't even been here long enough for her daddy to know her touch, and for her to know him. *How could God do this to Agnes? How could He take her away from her first grandbaby? How could He do this to Gianni? How could He deny her knowing, learning from, and loving her grandmother?"* Mamma Greene was a woman who had lived most of her adult life serving God and raising their children to be God-fearing. *And this is how she is being repaid?* My emotions were running the gamut and I just couldn't comprehend what was going on.

Arnold's Heart

I knew I had to be strong for the family, and intellectually I knew that if God chose to take Ma, there was a reason ... but I was not ready for that. I was in such a struggle with my feelings and my faith. It didn't make sense that God would take her away from Gianni. As a youngster, I would often only look, selfishly, at how a crisis would affect me. I found myself questioning why God would put my daughter at the disadvantage of not knowing her grandmother and learning from her. For the first time in my life, I was angry with God. But as I drove up to Philadelphia, I felt at peace.

The ride was therapeutic. I had the opportunity to be alone with God and my thoughts. And I was able to reminisce. I thought about how my mother is truly the "perfect mother." Okay, everyone might say this about their mom, but they don't have Agnes as a mother. I thought about all of the petty arguments we'd had in the past. But I realized, now, how important she was to me. Sometimes it takes traumatic experiences in life to give us perspective on what is important and what is not.

The car was filled with my favorite compilation of music blasting at a deafening level. It seemed like I made the one-and-a-half-hour ride in fifteen minutes. The Acura Legend and I were s-p-e-e-d-i-n-g! I desperately wanted to get to New York. I admit I cried and lip-synched all the way to Philly. When I reached Tracey's house, almost before I put the car in park, she was in the passenger seat and we were on our way home.

Tracey's Heart

When Arnold arrived, we shared a hug. We were relieved at the fact that, up until that point, Ma had survived. The long ride to New York was filled with mixed emotions. Even though I was optimistic, I was still afraid. I found myself tearing up at the thought that she was at the brink of death. What haunted me most was not how I would have responded if God had taken her unto Himself, but what I would have regretted not saying or doing while she was alive. It was comforting and refreshing to know I could talk and actually be vulnerable with my "big brother." I thank God, because I couldn't have shared those frail moments with anyone better than Arnold.

Arnold's Heart

During the drive home, my resident comedienne, Tracey Greene, entertained me with her hilarious jokes. I guess she knew I needed to laugh. And laugh we did! She is a wonderful sister and friend. We shared some deep feelings with each other and went through our plan of support for Ma and Daddy. We arrived at the hospital in record time. Daddy met us in the lobby. We shared a moment of relief. And then came the tough part.

Tracey's Heart

I could tell from the hug Daddy shared with me and Arnold that he was comforted to have his whole family together. However, I couldn't keep the thought from racing through my mind, *But for how long?*

Doneisha's Heart

Deep down inside, I was bitter. The craziest thing is that I don't know whom or what it was that I felt caused the bitterness. I think I was partly bitter toward God and partly bitter toward the situation. This might sound really bizarre, but I think that I was even a little bitter and disappointed in "Mama Greene." Here I was in Maryland with our new baby girl and my husband was hundreds of miles away at the bedside of his critically ill mother. I felt cheated.

Suddenly, something hit me like a ton of bricks as I struggled to sort out my feelings and all that was swirling around us. I call the moment "Doneisha's Epiphany." God simply said to me, "Doneisha, she is human! She is not invincible." I accepted the correction in my head. But my heart was screaming, "Whatever!"

Arnold's Heart

The two-minute walk to Ma's room was the longest I had ever taken. As I peered into her room, expecting the worst, I could hear her talking. Initially, I thought it was my imagination, but sure enough, it was Ma! In an animated tone, she was talking to our cousin, Bettye, as she fell in and out of sleep. I almost broke down because this was so unlike her, but I composed myself as I approached her bed. It was so difficult to see my mother lying there so heavily medicated. But when she saw Tracey and me, she said, "Arnold, Tracey, what are you doing here? I am all right!" I felt then that my strong mother was going to be with me for years to come. Yes, indeed, God *does* do all things well.

Tracey's Heart

As I watched Ma in the hospital room, I breathed a sigh of relief and thought "Hallelujah! She is really alive!" But at the same time I thought, "Oh God, I've never seen her this way!" I was filled with mixed emotions. Her face was swollen, lips ashen, and hair matted. *Ma's hair matted?* Her hair was always neat, even on a bad-hair day! Though she recognized me, there was a void that she usually filled with the grace that only my mother could display.

Yes, I was relieved to see her awake and responsive, but when she spoke it was as if a child was before me. And this didn't make any sense because *I was* the child! *How could a woman so full of strength, wisdom, grace, kindness, love, and life be so quickly reduced to a babe?* What I was really thinking inside was, *If Ma is in this condition, who is going to change my diapers, feed me, sew my pretty dresses for church, straighten my hair, iron my clothes, cook turkey wings, pick me up from tennis practice, help me type papers all night, nag me about my room being messy, make me wash the dishes, deal with my adolescent attitudes, rip the lead to "I Can Go To God In Prayer,"*—and on, and on.

I was twenty-two at the time, but I felt like a baby being weaned, instantly, from my loving mother's nipples. Where did the time go between my perfect childhood and now? There was such a roller coaster of emotions funneling through me. I just didn't understand how our family could seem so complete a week and a half ago at Gianni's birth and now, everything we had to be happy about was suddenly being stripped away. Now my mother was like a baby.

How could the same woman who remembered every fact and caught me in lies, now not remember who was standing in front of her just moments before? I tried to hold myself together and appreciate the gift of her life. But eventually, I broke down and began to cry. I just didn't understand what God could be doing here.

Doneisha's Heart

After some time with myself, I began to understand why I'd had those bitter feelings toward my mother-in-law. I think the world of Agnes Greene—I always have and always will. My problem was that I had her on a pedestal so high, you would have thought her to be a superhero. Here was this strong, intelligent, dynamic woman who seemed to be almost invincible. She was active and healthy. She had had her annual physical the day before and received a clean bill of health from her doctor. And now, she was in the hospital, in a coma, after having a seizure? How could that be?

Just five days before, she'd been with us in Maryland, holding and kissing her granddaughter, changing diapers—all the while proclaiming that Gianni was the prettiest baby she had ever seen. (As any grandmother worth her salt would say). *How could superwoman allow this to happen at such a wonderful time in our lives?*

Arnold's Heart

After days of testing, a tumor was discovered on my mother's brain. And right in line with her famous statement, "God does all things well," the doctor said the tumor was in the "best possible site" on the brain. But what could that mean? Now I know. As God would have it, the only effect the tumor has had on her is that she has a tremendous testimony of the healing power of God.

She has become one of my best friends, evidenced by the fact that I speak to her at least three times a week as she questions, "Am I your girlfriend?" in her sassy and humorous tone. I have grown so much through this experience. But Ma, the next time you decide to pattern your hairstyle after mine, just know you don't have to resort to such drastic measures!

I won't write much more because it has taken me long enough to get this close to the end. In fact, sharing this writing has been therapeutic. Actually, this is the first time I allowed myself to recount any of the events. As a result, I have been able to release some of the pain I experienced during my mother's illness. I would never acknowledge how much my very being ached. Therefore, I couldn't release the pain until now. I could not even bear to look at any pictures of her from the "good old days." But I realize now that these *are* her best days. Boy, have I cried while recounting the details! And I feel so much better now. Ma, after all is said and done, I want you to know I love you very, very dearly.

You have been asking me to complete this writing for a while and it has taken everything in me to do so. My prompting came on June 12, 2001, when I learned that a young man I'd hired about five months before had passed away. I can remember speaking with him on Friday, June 1, regarding his scheduled surgery on June 5 to remove a brain tumor. He had the surgery, but, unfortunately, he didn't recover. I decided to finish this writing because the fact of the matter is things could have been very different for our family.

And so I've shared from my heart. Our family has a lot to be thankful for and I can truly say God does all things well! Loving you always —I am your number one son.

Doneisha's Heart

So many times, I have attempted to write down what I experienced emotionally, mentally, and physically after Mama Greene lapsed into a coma. But I would always find an excuse for not doing so. The first thing I had to examine was why writing this was so difficult. Then I realized that, as a family, we had never discussed how we felt about the situation. We never talked about how this event had affected our lives individually. We sort of went on with life, celebrating the miracle. I tried to talk to Arnold about it one day. I was commenting about how extremely blessed we were to have his mother still here with us. Not once did he look me in the face. He just said, "Yes we are, and I don't want to talk about it again!"

Mama Greene, you are truly loved and adored. You might not be a superhero, but you are our family's superwoman! Thank you for hounding me to write about this experience. The writing has actually turned into therapy for me. The irony of it all is that I didn't realize how much I was still hurting and that there were unresolved issues I needed to address. Thank you for allowing me to share. My healing has begun! I love you much!

Tracey's Heart

As the week continued, I learned the value of friends, loved ones, and the saints who prayed diligently. Most of all, I came to value my family in a way that I never did before. However, I had to come to the realization and accept that Ma could suffer from long-term side effects of brain trauma. But, certainly, she would still be who God has ordained her to be!

Once the rawness of my emotions and pain subsided, I was forced to acknowledge what God was trying to say to me. First, from the heart of one mother's child to you, I urge you to continually "honor [your] father and mother; that [your] days may be long upon the land which the Lord [your] God has given you" (Exodus 20:12). This commandment from God is one that we must practice and improve upon daily. Many of the sayings that I heard growing up, now ring true and clear. They aren't simply words—no longer just clichés. Sometimes, it takes almost losing what is most valuable for you to realize its true worth.

Secondly (on a personal note), the spirit of God challenged me to evaluate my relationship with God. During this time, I became keenly aware of my need to determine whether I was taking the welfare of my soul for granted. The challenge that this whole event issued to me was to know God's place in my life and to find my place in God. The morals of the story: Never leave the answering machine and the phone off and "God is sovereign, I am nothing." Since God can and will do what He wants, the key question is, how will we respond? Ma, I love you eternally.

Chapter Three
Sisters Lookin' Out

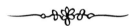

During the entire event of my illness and recovery, I saw God develop and mature my extended family, particularly my sisters. I watched them transition from having a relationship of acquaintance with God to an intimate relationship with God.

I am one of ten siblings (two brothers and eight sisters). We were brought up to love, respect, and look out for one another. Don't get me wrong, we weren't "goody-two-shoes" by any stretch of the imagination. During our former years, we had our share of bickering, fussing, and siding one against the other. But our father and mother did not allow us to mistreat or mishandle each other. For the most part, though, we had big-time fun growing up. Besides, we didn't have much idle time because there was plenty of work to do on our farm. Daddy was no easy taskmaster, and he made sure we gained a work ethic—whether we wanted to or not. Now all aging adults (the youngest at fifty-three years old and the oldest, eighty years old), we still enjoy each other's company and value each other's counsel. Despite the challenges our family has faced, God has helped us to weather the storms together. It then stood to reason that, when this storm hit, my sisters, particularly, were there at the ready. They were an integral part of my physical, emotional, and spiritual healing. My siblings and I have differing circumstances, which heighten the complexities of who we are, but there are common threads that weave us together. These threads are the love and respect that we have for each other and the reverence and love we have *for God. We are so blessed to have been recipients of excellent teaching by two excellent role models. They wove godly values into the tapestry of our lives and these guiding principles remain at our core.*

Though my brothers are an integral part of my life, I am especially grateful to have seven wonderful sisters. At the time of my illness and recovery, my sisters lived in four different states and had their own family responsibilities. But Jerry and I were privileged to have one or more of them with us for four weeks, lending their hands and giving us their love and support. Nothing compares to the nurturing spirit of a woman. These women are my sisters by birth, but my friends—my "sistah-girls"— by choice. Thanks, sisters (Saretter, Edna, Chars, Betty, Minnie, Ponzella and Alphenia) for being there and looking out for me! Read now as each of them shares her feelings about the experience. —AG

"Helping Hands"

Saretter, a.k.a. Sister

When I received the news about Agnes's illness, I was shocked, to say the least. Then I became afraid! Immediately, I was reminded and so thankful that God had allowed sixty-two years to pass without breaking our brother-sister circle. Yet I could only think of death. I cried and I prayed, and I cried and I prayed some more. I thought to myself, *Agnes has been a good girl. She yielded her life to Christ early in her youth and has lived for the Lord, completely. She seemed to always be in tune with God, with her body, her mind, and her spirit. Agnes didn't drink, smoke, curse, or do some of the things many young people get involved in. She was obedient to our parents and her older siblings, courteous to everyone, and so in love with Jesus Christ. And now she lies seriously ill.* I continued to cry and pray: *What will happen to her children?* Although they were adults, my heart was broken for them. I also thought about her husband, Jerry. Somehow I felt he was better equipped to deal with the situation than Arnold and Tracey were. I wanted so much to be there for her, but she was so far away.

Then I remembered the scripture (Philippians 4:6), where the Bible teaches us that we are to be anxious for nothing, but by prayer and supplication, we are to make our request known to God. I called my prayer partners: my pastor and our first lady. Then I called other church members, asking them to be in constant prayer for Agnes and her family. We prayed. Some of us fasted.

My first conversation with God was very serious. It ended with, "God, You made Agnes and You molded her. We love her and don't want You to take her from us. Now, if it is Your will that she lives a while longer, please heal her and continue to use her for Your Glory! I believe that she will be what You want her to be and do what You want her to do. But if You see fit to take her home with You, somehow let her know how much we love her. In all, we thank You for the time You have loaned her to us." Then I tried to take solace in the scripture, John 11:4, in which, after Lazarus died, Jesus said "*...this sickness is not unto death, but for the glory of God, that the Son of God might be glorified thereby.*"

Today, I think often about Agnes's illness and the miraculous way in which God healed her. I still continue to pray and thank God for all of His blessings. I thank God that this experience opened the eyes and hearts of many of our family members. Agnes is still being prayed for and asked about. I have commended her into the hands of the Almighty God, knowing that He is able to take perfect care of her.

Chars, a.k.a. Cha'

I was lying in bed when Betty called and told me that Agnes had seizures and was in a coma, and the situation looked bleak. Immediately, I got out of bed and began praying. "Not now, Lord, not now!" I pleaded with God not to take Agnes from us. My mind went back to the time when my husband, Charles, had had a massive stroke and lapsed into a coma. I can still remember how helpless I felt. I wondered how Jerry, Arnold, and Tracey were doing.

When I told Charles what happened, he was in total disbelief and expressed much sadness. He doesn't talk much, but he is very fond of Agnes. The first call I made was to my pastor. I shared with him what happened and asked him to lift Agnes up before the Lord in prayer. I began calling everyone I could think of, asking them to pray for Agnes. I called pastors of other churches in the community, asking that they and their congregations pray. My faith in God and my belief in the divine power of the Holy Spirit is very real. But to be honest, I did question God, asking, "Lord, why Agnes?" Agnes gave her life to God at an early age and was a shining example for all of us. She was faithful to God and her family. I kept thinking about what would happen to her husband and her children, in particular, if she was called to be with her Maker.

My experiences in the "wilderness" have helped me to truly realize that God is wise and does all things well. I began to reflect on some of the difficult times in my life: when I contracted tuberculosis, when my husband suffered a massive stroke, leaving him paralyzed, and when I helped to care for our parents, who were stricken with chronic and terminal illnesses, for over ten years. As a result of the mental and emotional stress of being one of their primary caregivers, I became disabled in 1991. But through it all, God sustained me! I know it was God's grace and mercy that elevated me to another level of faith during these experiences. Therefore, I was able to trust God for Agnes, knowing that He is perfect in all of His doings.

Ponzella, a.k.a. Pomp

When Cha' called me early on Saturday morning and told me that Agnes was critically ill, I was in total shock. I tossed and turned for a while, not able to go back to sleep. Finally, I rolled out of bed, made a cup of coffee, and got dressed for my morning walk.

Just as I got back in the house with my newspaper, the phone rang. It was Chars calling again to say it didn't look good for Agnes. For some reason, I knew I still needed to go to the track. I didn't think I would have the strength to get around the track, but I went anyway. As I walked, praying for Agnes, I suddenly felt a wonderful sense of peace. Now that I felt God was in action, I headed home and began some chores. It may seem odd, but as I moved around the house, I kept thinking that soon I would receive the call saying Agnes was all right. But when the third call came, it wasn't the news I wanted to hear. Chars told me that Agnes's condition was declining and encouraged me to continue praying. As I knelt down beside my bed, I found myself stretched out, face down on the floor. It was as if I was *pulled* into that position. I don't remember saying anything. What I felt was a "bucketful" of tears pouring from my eyes. I didn't question God; I didn't think I had a right. I pulled myself up and sat on the edge of the bed. Shortly thereafter, I became overwhelmed with a wonderful sense of peace again, just as I had at the track.

I've never told Agnes, but I've watched her from a distance over the years and she has taught me, by example, what it means to *live* a Christian life. Agnes's life has been a godly road map, if you will. In my own private time, I continued to pray for Agnes's health and well-being.

Alphenia, a.k.a. Phenia

Saturday, March 21 began like any other day. I was up and about doing my household chores when the phone rang. When I answered, I heard Jerry say, "Phenia … Agnes is very sick!" He continued, "She had seizures last night and it doesn't look good." He told me that she was admitted to the hospital and was in a coma. Then he said words I'll never forget: "Y'all need to come to New York, as soon as possible."

After hanging up the phone, I remember staring at the wall, in total disbelief. It just didn't seem real to me. Suddenly, I fell on my knees and asked God to please let my sister live. I can remember repeating that, over and over again, crying uncontrollably. Then, just as quickly as I started crying, I felt an unbelievable peace and calm envelop me. I knew then, without a doubt, that my prayer was answered.

Later that day, my sisters and I caught a bus to New York. Jerry picked us up from the bus station. As we rode to the hospital, he began telling us what had happened the night before. The ordeal sounded like something ripped from the pages of a novel. But I knew that God would decide how the "story" ended. When we reached the hospital and entered Agnes's room, she greeted us with a smile and a "hey yah!" But she appeared a little "out of it." She kept talking, but not nearly as much as usual. She had a puzzled look on her face as if she was confused about what had just recently happened. During our stay with Agnes, I told her how much I loved her and that I was praying for her.

Minnie Bell, a.k.a. Minnie

I sort of swept the news of Agnes's illness under the rug after hanging up the phone with Betty. You see, we have a cousin who has a long history of seizures and after his episodes, he seemed to bounce back. As a result, I didn't think Agnes's response would be any different. Jerry was in touch with Betty, and she kept me posted. The first few hours after Betty told me the news, I was kind of laid back. I didn't think there was much to be terribly concerned about. But Jerry kept calling, so I decided it was time to get up off my "duff" and go see about her. Even when my sisters and I arrived at the hospital and saw Agnes, the severity of her condition still did not resonate with me. Although she appeared a little tired and "worn out," I thought she looked "pretty okay."

However, after spending some time with her and hearing the details of her "near-death" encounter, I knew that this was serious. I don't recall exactly when I was told that she had a brain tumor and would require surgery, but I knew then it was time to do some serious praying. This was a confusing and trying time for me. I had recently committed my life to the Lord and was just beginning to know Him intimately. Somehow, it was hard for me to understand why God would "punish" someone that loved Him and served Him so diligently. I found myself spending a lot of time talking to God and asking questions. Not because I thought Agnes needed me to vouch for her. After all, she had been talking to Him well over half her life. But *I* needed to know I could trust God. So I began talking to God on her behalf because I knew she had to concentrate on preserving her strength. In fact, there were plenty of prayer warriors on the battlefield praying with us while Agnes rested.

Betty, a.k.a. BJ, a.k.a. "Luke the Physician"

I can still remember, vividly, the call I received early Saturday morning,

March 21, 1998. I had slept late and was just getting up when the phone rang. My sister, Cell, was on the line. She was hyperventilating. Trying to maintain her composure, she nervously told me that she had just received a call from her sister-in-law, Gladys. Agnes was in the hospital and her condition was critical. More specifically, she was classified as comatose. At that point, I went numb. It was as if time stood still. I was operating in slow motion. I didn't have the strength to get up from bed.

About an hour later, Cell called back to say that Gladys had contacted her again. This time she reported that though Agnes was still unconscious, her condition seemed to have improved. At that point, I attempted to reach Jerry, but there was no answer at their home. Then I called Jerry's sister, Geraldine, to find out what was going on. In a reassuring voice, she told me that Agnes was indeed in the hospital and had been classified as "critical." Geraldine went on to say that Agnes had regained consciousness and was beginning to recognize immediate family members. Her condition was upgraded to stable, and she was being transferred from the emergency room to a regular floor.

During our conversation, Geraldine related the series of events that had taken place since Agnes's sudden illness and said she believed people's prayers were answered on Agnes's behalf. She shared that when Jerry called to tell her what happened, she immediately informed her husband, Bishop Roderick Caesar, Sr. and then she fell to her knees and prayed. Sometime later, she contacted Rose Parris and asked her to pray and to call other prayer warriors from Bethel, Agnes and Jerry's former church. She then called her nephew, Terry, and her cousin, Bettye, and asked them to go and be with Jerry at the hospital.

After my conversation with Geraldine, I was finally able to mobilize myself. I told my husband, Thomas, about Agnes's illness. Then I started to contact my sisters in Maryland, New Jersey, North Carolina, and South Carolina. I told them that I was going to New York to be with Agnes. Thomas's initial response was that I should wait to hear from Jerry regarding Agnes's status. Finally, I reached Jerry late Saturday afternoon. He reassured me that Agnes's condition seemed to be improving and suggested that I wait before coming. So I decided not to go on Saturday night, but my spirit was very restless.

Early Sunday morning, I called Jerry and he told me Agnes was alert and responsive. We discussed my plans to drive up but he said it had snowed overnight and he did not think it was feasible to drive. At that point, I decided that I was taking the bus. I contacted Minnie and Phenia and suggested that we travel together. Thomas drove Minnie and me to New Jersey, where we connected with Phenia and boarded the bus to New York.

We arrived at the Port Authority bus terminal at about 9:30 Sunday night and waited for Jerry. As fate would have it, we kept overlooking Jerry and he kept overlooking us. It was about eleven that night before we finally bumped into each other. Jerry took us directly to the hospital, as we were eager to see Agnes. She was asleep when we arrived at the hospital at 12:20 am. We decided not to wake her, as she seemed to be resting comfortably. But apparently she was aroused by our presence, because she opened her eyes not long after we were settled in the room. It was obvious to us that she had been through a very traumatic experience. She was coherent and spoke appropriately but her language and motor skills were v-e-r-y slow. This may not have been significant for most people, but if you knew Agnes, you knew this was not normal. God had endowed her with the gift of communication and she used it well!

I had already decided ahead of time that I wasn't going to leave her bedside that night, and Jerry looked like he so desperately needed sleep. So after spending some time at the hospital, Jerry, Minnie, and Phenia left for home. Agnes rested quite well during the night, drifting in and out of sleep. When she did awaken, she wanted to talk, and talk we did! It was early morning when we both finally succumbed to sleep after an exhausting day and night.

I was encouraged Monday morning when Agnes asked the nurse if she could get out of the bed. The nurse gave us permission and I assisted her to the bathroom. She washed her face, brushed her teeth, returned to bed, and ate a hearty breakfast. Later that morning, I started her bed bath. As I was about to help her with her private area, I asked, "Do you want me to wash your *tush*?" She roared out a hearty laugh and said, "No, I will take care of my *own* tush." She proceeded to stand up by her bed and took care of her "independent self." I can recall thinking to myself, "She is going to be all right!"

As the day progressed, Agnes started to get a steady stream of visitors. And to my surprise and pleasure, she recognized everyone as they engaged in conversation. By this time, Jerry, Tracey, Minnie, and Phenia had returned to the hospital. One of her visitors, a pastor, ministered briefly to Agnes in private, and afterward asked to have prayer with the family. We all joined hands—what a powerful prayer! The atmosphere was spiritually charged. We knew and believed that God heard our prayers and would continue to respond to our needs.

Later that day, as Agnes was being transported for a CAT scan, we ran into one of the emergency room nurses. She was on duty when Agnes was brought in the night before. From the look on her face, I could tell that she did not believe Agnes was still alive. She kept staring at Agnes. Finally, she asked, "Are you the Mrs. Greene who was in the emergency room early Saturday morning?" Jerry answered, "Yes." She shook her head in disbelief and responded, "If I had not seen you in the emergency room with my own eyes, I would never believe that you could still be alive." She wished Agnes a speedy recovery and went on her way, still shaking her head with a puzzled look on her face.

Minnie and Phenia had to return home that day, so Jerry took them back to the bus station. Once he got back to the hospital, we stayed with Agnes until late evening. Agnes assured us that she would be okay and insisted that we go home early and get some rest. On our way home, we stopped by Geraldine's and enjoyed a delicious dinner before "crashing" in our cozy beds.

Tuesday, March 24—Agnes called to tell us that she was being transferred to another hospital that was better equipped to handle her next phase of treatment. Jerry and I threw on our clothes and sped to the hospital. It seemed like we were always on "fast forward." We got to the hospital in the nick of time, as Agnes was already on the stretcher, strapped in, and ready for the transport. We said our good-byes and extended our thanks to the staff for their care of Agnes. Then, off we drove to North Shore Medical Center.

The remainder of the day was spent checking in, meeting new staff, and obtaining preliminary assessments by the Chief of Neurology—trying to determine the next steps. We spent most of the day sitting around and waiting, which was a little unnerving. Agnes continued to have many visitors and a steady flow of telephone inquiries. She remained alert and chatty, but she would complain, from time to time, that she felt dizzy and wobbly. As a result, she was maintained on complete bed rest. We stayed until early evening and finally left for home, at her insistence.

Wednesday was another day of waiting for further assessments and tests. By the afternoon, we were becoming impatient and feeling a bit testy. So Jerry requested a meeting with the nursing supervisor and the social service staff. Later in the afternoon, we had discussions with people from both areas, who informed us that they would get in touch with the neurosurgeon who was handling Agnes's case. Jerry made it very clear that we were displeased with such a slow response. Also, Agnes's nurse informed us that her Dilantin level was extremely high. She was taking Dilantin to help control her seizure activities. I believe this may have contributed to her feeling off balance.

After visiting hours, we left the hospital, had dinner at Geraldine's again, and retired for the evening. About eleven o'clock, Agnes's "guardian angel," Thelma, called Jerry with some distressing news. She happened to make a late-night visit to the hospital and found Agnes, alone in her bathroom, crying. It seems that after Jerry and I left the hospital, she was told by the on-call resident neurologist that she needed to have surgery. This was very overwhelming for her to deal with alone! *Well*, this "pissed" Jerry off! Once again we raced to the hospital in the middle of the night. The minute we entered the lobby, I could sense that Jerry was ready for a battle. He was just looking for the target. And from what we were told, Thelma had *already* given the resident a pretty good tongue-lashing before we arrived. Jerry made it perfectly clear to the night nurse that by no means was anyone to have any conversation with Agnes unless he was present. We got Agnes settled, assuring her that this would never happen again. Not long after she fell asleep, we decided to leave for home.

You will never guess what happened next. Somehow, Jerry and I misunderstood each other's plan for the night. He left the room first and thought I was staying at the hospital with Agnes for the night. A short while later, I went downstairs, thinking he would be waiting for me in front of the lobby with the car. After waiting in the lobby for about forty-five minutes, I became alarmed and requested security to go look for his car. They returned and reported that they could not find his car after checking both parking lots. It suddenly dawned on me that he might have gone home. On a hunch, I called their home and sure enough, he was already home in bed, and he sounded as if he was already in REM sleep. The poor, tired man had to make another trip *back* to the hospital to pick me up. By now, we were bone-tired, but did we have a big chuckle as we replayed the scene.

Thursday, March 26—Dr. L. sauntered into Agnes's room at approximately 3:00 pm. He had such a cool, calm, and almost nonchalant demeanor about him. "Hi, I am Dr. L.," he said. Relieved to see him and with no disrespect intended, I shot back, "Well, it is about time! We have been waiting for you for two days!" He just smiled—I guess he understood the anxiety and the tension we were experiencing. After the introductions, he immediately started to discuss his findings. He said that the results of the tests from the current and prior hospitals confirmed a lesion on the left frontal lobe of Agnes's brain, which would require surgery. He explained further that if there was a good place to have a tumor, Agnes's tumor was in the best location. We requested a second brain scan and he agreed to order another test. When the doctor left, Agnes broke down and started to cry. This was so unusual because until this point, Agnes seemed to be handling everything very well. Tracey and I began to pray, and we also started to cry with her. And as Jerry continued to pray, Agnes started to pray in an indiscernible language. I can remember not being afraid but feeling so much pain for her.

Friday, March 27—Jerry and I returned to the hospital mid-morning. Agnes was already dressed for the day and in good spirits.

She didn't complain about anything. I recall her saying, again, that she didn't want to have the surgery but if it was her only option, she would go through with it. She had to undergo a battery of tests over the weekend, as surgery was scheduled for Monday, March 30. I left for Maryland that weekend and made plans to return to New York on the day of Agnes's surgery.

Edna, a.k.a. Cell

Imagine how quickly a helium-filled balloon deflates when it is punctured by an object. So, too, did my strength, as I listened to a voice on the telephone, in the early morning of March 21. *"Cell, this is Gladys. Are you all right? I'm calling because I've been told that Agnes is in critical condition."* The call was from my sister-in-law. For a moment, I felt as if everything inside me shut down, except tears. I remember falling to my knees, immediately, asking God to cover my sister with His blood, to be merciful to her and not let her die.

You see Agnes, like Mom and Dad, was a source of strength for me. You could count on her to offer sound advice and bring humor to any situation, even during a crisis. Her ability to offer positive solutions to problems and stimulate your thought process was one of her special gifts. She would say, "What if," or, "Think of it this way," or, "It could have been worse." It just didn't make sense that someone who offered mending and healing could now be the one who needed mending and healing.

When I learned of her illness, I had questions. What happened? Why her? I just knew it had to be the result of an automobile accident because, I thought, *Agnes was always in good health.* But even if it was not an accident, it still seemed untimely and unjustified. For as long as I can remember, Agnes always had a compassionate nature, loved the Lord, and encouraged others to choose the Ark of Safety, the Kingdom of God.

While en route from North Carolina to Maryland to link up with Betty and Minnie, I concentrated on preparing myself to be a pillar for Agnes. I read this passage from a *Daily Word* booklet: "The Holy

Spirit not only comforts us in times of stress and anxiety, He steadies us by remaining at our side and embracing us with the powerful loving affirmation of God. Whatever we are facing, we can be sure that God is facing it with us."

When we reached the hospital, I began to feel an overwhelming sense of anxiety as I entered the building and began walking through the corridors. I observed patients in their rooms: some calm, some crying, some staring into space, some anxiously walking the floor. *"What is Agnes doing?* I wondered. I wanted so much to hear her famous greeting, "Hey, Cellie Girl!" Instead, I got a warm smile and saw her reassuring eyes. Immediately she stated, "I know I will be all right." I thought, *of course you will! Haven't we always been taught and admonished to think positive and to believe that all things work together for good for those who love the Lord?* Yes, there are measures we must take to bring our wellness into fruition. We must acknowledge God for who He is, pray for His intervention, give Him praise and thanksgiving, have confidence in the ability of the medical staff, and then trust God for victory. God can and will bring restoration and healing to our bodies.

I rejoice and will be forever grateful for the network of love and support given to Agnes by her family and friends and loved ones from around the world. We must never underestimate the power of prayer, for the Word of God says that the effectual and fervent prayer of the righteous avails much. When we understand the dynamics of intercessory prayer and think about its effect, our response will be "Yea and Amen and to God be the glory!"

I was extremely grateful to God for Agnes's husband, Jerry, as I watched him demonstrate total dedication to our sister. With his loving spirit, he saw to every facet of care-giving. This, combined with his gifted ability to command calmness, provided an atmosphere for Agnes's plea, as she would sing, again and again, "When the storms of life are raging, Lord stand by me!"

Throughout this experience, Agnes demonstrated a strong faith in God, but there were times when her humanity surfaced as she expressed a fear of dying. She would say, "I'm not afraid of dying; I just want to live a little longer. I have some things I need to do. I have GiGi, our beautiful new granddaughter, who needs me to spend time with her and teach her some things about God and life."

There were times when I knew Agnes was in pain, but she would, somehow, try to make me feel comfortable and at ease in my effort to encourage her. Instead of being the encourager, I was encouraged by her faith. She has such a way of taking the attention off of herself and deflecting it onto others. She would say, repeatedly, "You don't know how much your being here means to me." But I did. Without our saying it, there was a shared feeling that resonated between the two of us, as we held on to God's blessed assurance, "I will never leave nor forsake you." And we stood firmly on that promise!

I was not angry, but I did question God as to why this was happening to someone who trusted and served Him. Agnes answered this question beautifully, as she, repeatedly, read the Word of God, saying, "Though He slay me, yet I trust God."

Agnes, Cellie Girl loves you!

Betty

Sunday, March 29—Minnie, Cell, and I made the trip back to New York by car. After getting lost a few times, Jerry came to the rescue, again! We arrived at the hospital about 5:00 pm. There, we found many of Agnes's and Jerry's long-time friends from church and other walks of life by her side. Their friends were steadily praying with and for her and continuously providing support. I know that God surrounded Agnes with many "angels." At the time, Cell was experiencing excruciating back pain, but God enabled her to endure through this stressful time.

Monday, March 30—the day of surgery was upon us, and we all prepared ourselves privately for what we, particularly Agnes, were about to face. I was lying in bed praying when I touched my right eye and realized that I was experiencing a flare-up of my iris. I responded, "O my

God, not now!" At that moment, I told the devil, "You won't distract me now!" So I put on my dark sunglasses and off we went to the hospital.

When we reached the hospital, Agnes was very upbeat. She seemed the strongest of us all. After a series of pre-surgical brain scans and an unexpected delay, we finally returned to Agnes's room. By now, it was about two hours before surgery was scheduled to begin. Agnes began a prayer by reading us a scripture that God had directed her to the previous night—Psalm 118:17. It read: "I will not die but live to tell of the goodness of the Lord." Then Jerry, Arnold, Tracey, other family members, and some close friends entered into a corporate prayer for Agnes, the surgical team, and the supporting surgical staff.

After prayer, Agnes committed herself and the surgery to God. Then, Jerry, Arnold, Tracey, and I accompanied her to the surgical wing. We all shared hugs, kisses, and tears. We told her that we would be praying and waiting to see her after surgery. Her stretcher and our hearts rolled through the doors of the operating room. And we were all left to sit, wonder, and pray.

Minnie

The hardest time for me, during the ordeal, was the wait while Agnes was in surgery. Those were the longest and most difficult hours in my life. I asked God questions like "Lord, Agnes has been your servant every since I can remember, so why in the world would You want to take her?" and remonstrated, "Agnes has done nothing but try to win souls to You." God was silent. It seemed like God was intentionally not answering my question, "Why Agnes?" but trying to help me understand, "Why not Agnes?" I recognized that I had absolutely no grounds to question Him. After all, she was His servant. So I said, "Okay, Lord, I have no more questions."

When the surgery was over, Jerry and Betty came back to the room to tell us that everything had gone well and that Agnes was resting. But for whatever reason, I still had some reservations and wanted to see her with my own eyes to be sure. I don't remember how much time passed before we were able to see her but when I did, it was like my first taste of Breyers Ice Cream—and do I love Breyers!

I can remember feeling so relieved when I peeked through a small opening between the recovery room doors and saw Agnes's dazed eyes looking up at the ceiling. It looked as though Agnes, in her comical way, was saying to herself, "Thank you Lord!" or "Where in the heck am I?" She is so funny! It was at that moment that I knew God had answered our prayers and that He was still in the "Blessing Business." There is not much else that sticks out in my mind except that I am truly grateful that God decided *not yet!*

Agnes, I want you to know that I praise God every time I think of the grace and mercy that was extended to you—and us. I love you dearly!

Betty

After praying and waiting, we were informed that the surgery was over. The surgery lasted about eight hours—so we waited for word from the operating surgeon. But the call we were expecting never came. We found out later that the surgeon attempted to contact us, but the telephone in Agnes's room was swamped with calls from family and friends.

When we could wait no longer, a few of us set out to try to find the doctor. After combing the hospital, Jerry and I ran into Dr. L. by the nurses' station. He said he had tried to reach us (in Agnes's room), but the line was busy. He told us that the surgery was successful and that he felt very comfortable that the tumor was completely removed. He also said that the tumor was categorized as a "high 2 to a low 3 grade" on a rating of 1 to 4.

Jerry's immediate response was, "What does that mean?" The surgeon told us the tumor was malignant (cancerous) but they believed that all of the diseased tissue was removed. Instinctively, Jerry and I looked at each other and agreed we would not tell the family that part, at least, not yet. So we walked back into the room and Jerry announced to relieved family and friends that the surgery was successful. I know it was divine arrangement that the call we were expecting from Dr. L. did not come through to Agnes's room for everyone to hear. At the time, I don't believe that everyone could have handled that news.

As soon as we were allowed, we made our way to the recovery room for a short visit with Agnes. Jerry, Arnold, and Tracey went in first. Then, Minnie and I went in together. I was relieved to see Agnes awake, alert, and talking. One of my first instincts was to check for movement in her legs and feet. As I pulled the cover back and started feeling Agnes's toes, she asked, "Do I still have my polish on my toenails?" We all laughed, and I responded, "Yes, but more importantly, you can move your toes." At that point, I thought, *Thank You, God! If she can remember such a small detail immediately after eight hours of brain surgery, she will be okay."*

We were then encouraged by the hospital staff to go home, rest and return the next day. They assured us that they would call if there were any changes. We all left the hospital drained. And rest, we did!

Tuesday, March 31. We were up, "bright and shiny," getting ready to return to the hospital. The phone rang and Cell answered. I heard her asking, "Who? Who is this?" She then yelled out to us saying, "This is Agnes! This is Agnes! She's on the phone! She wants us to bring her toiletries when we come to the hospital." It was encouraging, but just so unbelievable that the day after having brain surgery, she would be able to ask for personal items with such clarity. I chuckled and said to them, "You know, we have been praying and asking God for a miracle. He has performed it before our very eyes and now we can hardly believe the miracle is happening. When we arrived, we were told that she would be transferred out of the recovery room to the step-down unit and not Intensive Care, as had been anticipated.

By the time we returned on Wednesday morning, April 1, Agnes was being prepared to move from the step-down unit to a regular room. That morning, she decided to show us the surgical incision. I watched her eyes as she searched our faces for a reaction. I think we did well. Arnold saved the day and made us all laugh when he said, "Ma, all you have to do now is cut off the rest of your hair and you will look just like me." Although Agnes had a clean incision site, I wondered how she would be affected, emotionally, by this life-changing event.

Later on that morning, Agnes was given the okay by her physical therapist to walk around the hall with assistance. I will remember this scene for a long time. As she walked down the hallway, proudly holding onto Jerry's arm, I noticed she was wearing a semi-sheer gown and a robe with no bloomers. She was just as excited as she could be! She didn't have a clue that her buns were on full display.

Even though Agnes had just gone through what most of us would have buckled under, God used Agnes that morning in such a wonderful way. After she returned to the room to put on her bloomers, she went to another patient's room to talk. The woman looked to be about sixty years old and was facing the same surgery that Agnes had just undergone. She stayed in that patient's room for so long that we had to go get her. This had become "the norm" for us because whenever the opportunity availed itself, Agnes would always share her faith in God.

Agnes was doing so well that Minnie and I decided to return home that day. Although Cell continued to be bothered with severe back pain, she decided to stay with Agnes through the weekend, until Chars could come to be with Agnes and Jerry. Minnie and I made plans to return every other weekend to visit Agnes and Jerry in April.

We knew we needed to continue to support and encourage Agnes during her recovery period. It was during one of our weekend visits that I watched Agnes, as she continuously exercised her faith in God and it literally rubbed off on me. One night, she was a little anxious and restless. She said she was tired but couldn't go to sleep. Finally, she asked me to anoint her with oil and pray. I felt stupid and ashamed as I had to confess, "I don't know how to anoint you." She took the bottle of oil from her nightstand, poured some in my hand, and said, "All you have to do is rub the oil on my head and pray for me, in the name of Jesus." So I did as instructed. God moved through me in a way I had never experienced before. Shortly afterward, Agnes relaxed and fell asleep. She even had the nerve to snore!

Minnie and I didn't see Agnes again until late May, when our family gathered for our niece's graduation celebration in New Jersey. Agnes looked great. She had decided to cut her hair and was wearing a short, natural style. Although she seemed a little withdrawn and reserved, she looked stunning. Everyone kept telling her how great she looked, and by the end of the day, I think she began to believe it.

During the events surrounding Agnes's surgery and recovery, I didn't give much thought about how Jerry was affected until I began writing these entries. Naturally, our focus (including his) was on Agnes's well-being—and rightly so. In hindsight, I can't imagine what a gut-wrenching ordeal this must have been for him. Jerry always seemed so upbeat and in control. I saw him cry only once. I witnessed how Agnes relied on him and drew from his tower of strength and his undaunted faith in God. He was a tremendous part of her healing process. I love him dearly and honor him for his strength and his unwavering love and protection of Agnes. He is God's gift to her!

Alphenia

On the day of Agnes's surgery, I started my day with prayer and I continued praying throughout the day. God did exactly what He said He would do—take care of His own. I was full of praise and thanksgiving to God when I received the news that Agnes came through surgery, and I continued to trust God to be in control of her healing process. As I watched her trust in God, my faith increased. I know that God can do more than anything that we can ask or think of Him. Our God is the awesome God!

Chars

After Agnes was discharged from the hospital, she needed someone to come and be with her for a while. I made arrangements with family members and friends to help take care of my husband while

I went to New York to stay with Agnes and Jerry for a month. I watched Agnes progress from using a portable toilet at the bedside to gradually walking to the bathroom with assistance. Her faith in God never wavered, and as a result, she began to grow stronger. Slowly, she attempted to walk up and down the stairs with my support. As time progressed, she became steadier. She just needed to know that someone was there. Any progress Agnes made, she would always give thanks and praise to God.

Because the hair on the left side of her head was shaved off for the surgery, I would brush and braid the right side. I tried to encourage her to cut all of her hair off so it would grow back evenly. Agnes struggled for a while with that reality, but finally she decided to go to her beautician. Her beautician reassured her that, in time, her hair would grow back stronger. When we got back home from the salon, Agnes looked in the mirror and said, "That does not look nearly as bad as I thought." Guess what? The praises to God went up once again!

Soon, Agnes began moving around the house more independently. Eventually, she was able to come to the table and share meals with the family. She loved to talk and witness, and as she regained her strength, she was able to entertain her visitors. Then Agnes and I ventured outside for some exercise. We started to walk, one block at a time.

As she gained strength, the walks began to get longer and longer. After only one week, she was able to walk ten blocks!

During the month that I spent with Agnes and Jerry, they encouraged me to witness to others about what God had done in my life. When I returned home, I began to witness, boldly, telling others about the joy it is to know and serve the Lord. God gave me the opportunity to tutor a twelve-year-old girl who was diagnosed with cancer. I shared my experiences and my belief and faith in God with her. One day, after our tutoring session, I prayed with her and invited her to commit her life to the Lord. She did and is now an ambassador for Christ! I owe much thanks to God for this "good seed" of faith that was sown in my spirit during my time with Agnes and her family.

I thank God for the privilege of ministering to them. In return, my spirit was ministered to in immeasurable ways. As a result of this experience, I have grown in my walk of faith and my ultimate goal, each day I live, is to win souls for Christ.

My New Outlook

GiGi and Nana	Tracey and Ma'

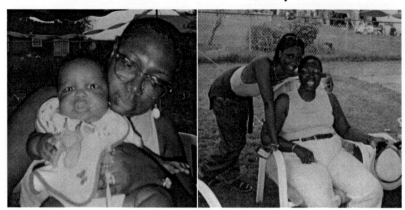

For the first two months during my recovery, my sisters Betty and Minnie (between whom I am sandwiched, in birth order) visited me and Jerry every other weekend. They knew I was struggling with my new "forced" hairdo. One weekend, I can remember Betty (the nurse) saying to me "I sense that you are struggling with an alteration in your self-esteem." This was her nursing way of saying, "I don't think you are comfortable with the way you look." I wanted to shoot back, in a not-so-nice- nursing way, "Well, would you be?" But I didn't. I knew she meant well. They later told me that during their early visits, I would not make eye contact with them.

I must admit that, before my surgery, I took great pride in the appearance of my hair. I thought of it as one of my better attributes. There are some women who showcase their hour-glass figures, others their well-endowed butts, while some show off their voluptuous breasts. But even on a "bad-hair" day, I gave special attention to the grooming and styling of my hair.

On one visit, Betty and Minnie arrived, announcing "We brought a special gift for you." Excitedly, I opened my gift bag. Inside, I found a wig that was a replica of my pre-surgery hair, both in style and texture! I will admit I was never a fan of wigs, but I was so elated that Betty and Minnie didn't buy me just any wig. They chose one they felt would compliment me, thus helping to maintain my sense of self.

I not only had to adjust to the new look that was thrust upon me, but I also wondered whether Jerry would be pleased with the "new me." You see, Jerry was accustomed to my shoulder-length "permed" hair. As a matter of fact, he would often tell me that one of the things that he found attractive about me was that my hair was always so well groomed.

On a second visit, Betty and Minnie arrived, announcing once again, "We have a special gift for you!" I responded, "Great, as long as you don't try to make me a blond or a redhead." Instead, they gave me a most beautiful pair of Afro-centric, hanging ivory earrings. I had never worn this type of earring before, but they were such a compliment to my new closely cropped "natural" hairstyle. My sisters also gave me a beautiful vase that has an endearing meaning to me. It is encircled by several women standing backward around the vase. Their hands are clasped in this backward position and their faces are looking away from the vase, as if they are on watch.

I've named this vase "Sisters Lookin' Out."

Chapter Four
An Attack or a Test?

———⚬✥⚬———

Many are the afflictions of the righteous:
but the Lord delivereth him out of them all.

Psalm 34:19 (KJV)

During the initial phase of my recovery, I was compelled to study the Book of Job. God knew I needed a remedial class in my understanding of Him, so He enrolled me in *Sovereignty 101* before I could continue to pursue "my major." During this study, I could sense a close parallel between Job's experience and mine. I would ask myself, "What is the lesson to be learned?" Three words repeatedly came to my mind: prologue, experience, and epilogue. As I studied and paralleled my circumstance with Job's, I gained insight into the significance of these words as they related to my encounter. The depth of my "prologue" relationship with God, juxtaposed with my "Job experience," was paramount in determining if my "epilogue" relationship with God would remain intact.

Job was a wealthy, healthy, righteous farmer who lived in biblical times. He was married and had a large family, lots of servants, and thousands of sheep, camel, and other livestock. Job was known as the richest cattleman in that land; he was a man of upright character, a man who feared and loved God. All was going well with him. Job's prologue (Job Chapters 1, 2) gives a poignant and vividly troubling account of how his wealth, health, family, and faith suffered a sudden and tragic attack. But in the epilogue (Chapter 42:7–17), we find solace. It was Job's faith in God that gave the story a comforting end.

> *Even though [Satan] intended to do harm ... God intended it for good.*
>
> Genesis 50:20 (NRSV)

I feel a special kinship with Job in my spirit. Like Job, suddenly and without warning, I was thrust face to face in an encounter with death! Remember, I had no warning of my impending illness. I did not have a history of seizures, nor did I experience any of the classic symptoms of having a brain tumor. Although I was listed as comatose in the natural world, somehow I knew that in the spiritual realm, God spoke to my spirit and would use this experience to rescue me from "shallow waters." He was fitting me for the "deeper waters" of my life's purpose.

> *Deep calleth unto deep at the noise of thy waterspouts ...*
> *Yet the Lord will command his loving kindness in the*
> *daytime, and in the night his song shall be with me ...*
>
> Psalm 42:7–8

God did not warn Job of the forthcoming calamities and great distress he would experience, nor did God forewarn me. Job could not believe the tragedies he had experienced and neither could I. Job's faith in God was tested and so was mine. Even at the strong chiding of his wife, he did not curse God, as she recommended: "Are you still trying to be godly when God has done all this to you? Curse him and die" (Job 2:9). But Job's reply was: "What? Shall we receive only pleasant things from the hand of God and never anything unpleasant?" (Job 3:10). Job did not curse God, but he cursed the day he was born. The Living Bible explains it this way:

> Job was experiencing extreme pain as well as grief over
> the loss of his family and possessions. He can't be blamed
> for wishing he were dead. Job's grief placed him at the

crossroads of his faith, shattering many misconceptions about God [promises] to make you rich, always keep you from trouble, or protects your loved ones. At [Job's] deepest point of despair, he was driven back to the basics of his faith in God. He only had two choices: (1) he could curse God and give up, or (2) he could trust God and draw strength from God to continue.

My faith, like Job's, was tested to the "max." I did not curse God, but the encounter left me with many questions. There were times when I came close to accusing God of not caring about me. My faith and fear were at war, in a "Tet Offensive-like battle." Jerry often talks about the Tet Offensive (the ultimate military strategy) that the North Vietnamese Army waged against the United States near the end of the Vietnam War. In their desperation to win, the North Vietnamese Army spared nothing. They utilized every available force that they could muster, including their women and children. There were times when it seemed like fear would win and overtake my faith, but thanks to God's grace and mercy, my faith ultimately won the battle!

In the process of my coming to know God's sovereignty, I had to grasp hold of and be reconciled with a very critical understanding. Though tragedy is often looked at as punitive, it is not always the consequence of personal sin. This is an extraordinarily difficult concept to embrace when you are in the "heat of the battle" because logic insists that we believe in the "cause and effect" theory. But when I was on the hot seat, it was critical to my recovery that I recognize that my illness was not a punishment. It was then that I learned an important lesson. I've entitled it "How to Be Careful Not to Sin While Suffering." You might ask, "What exactly does that mean? Well, when we find ourselves in difficult or hard places, we must not question the sovereign work of God by asking, "Why me?" or "Why am I experiencing this period of testing or trial?" Rather, we must seek to know who God is during the test and seek to understand what is to be learned from the experience.

The Hebrew word for *know*, in the context of intimacy or experience, is *yadah*. To yadah God is to embrace God as a fact, or as truth; to "take custody" with clarity and with certainty; to have a clearly developed and formulated faith; to have a fully expressed faith; to have a "nothing-implied" faith, an outspoken faith. Conversely, for one to know God by academia or hearsay, the Hebrew word used is *yada*. To yada God is to have a circumstantial faith in God, a by-chance or conditional faith in God.

Over and over again I dialogued with God, as did Job, trying to gain some level of appreciation of why I was experiencing what seemed like a tragedy. I gave the usual arguments: "God, I've strived to please you! I've tried to walk upright before you in the presence of my family, my neighbors, and even my enemies!" And, as if God didn't already know, I added, "I've been faithful to my husband. I've trained up my children, by word and deed, to love, fear and serve You! I've ... I've ... I've ... So why, God? Why? And I don't want to die now!"

Job asked God similar questions, just in a different language. God responded to Job by asking him a series of questions that no human could possibly answer (read Job 38–41). Job was in great distress and God's response seemed far from empathetic to Job's physical, emotional, and spiritual pain. As a matter of fact, God appeared to be mocking Job by asking him those questions, because He already knew Job didn't have the answers.

Can you picture the CEO of a company answering trivial questions from a new employee, such as: "Why is our work day from 8 am to 4 pm?" "Why do we only get forty-five minutes for lunch?" "Why do we celebrate only ten holidays per year, instead of twelve?" Expecting a CEO to respond to such "offensive" questions would not only be nonsensical, but highly unlikely. The answers to these questions were determined long before the new employee came aboard. If the employee values the company and the position he holds, he would be wise to settle down to the task of performing the job for which he was hired—and keep his mouth shut!

God didn't tell Job why He let him suffer. In an article entitled "The Great Debate," Mart DeHann offers this thought: "What [God] seemed to say was, 'Look at what I've done. Decide for yourself. Am I the kind of God who lacks power or wisdom or goodness? If I have done all that you see by the power and wisdom of My own Spirit, can you trust Me in the midst of the trouble I have allowed into your life?'" [2]

Did Job survive an *attack* or did he endure a *test*? I believe he experienced both, concurrently. These are two very important points that one must understand and distinguish when faced with a crisis. One's perception of the crisis will determine if one will be a victim of the attack or a victor of the test. Let's look at how they differ.

~

One's perception of the crisis will determine if one will be a victim of the attack or a victor of the test.

~

An *attack* is rendered by an enemy, whose sole purpose is to weaken, destroy, or kill. The enemy gives no warning of the attack, comes from out of nowhere, "plays dirty," and is, most often, camouflaged. This description can be likened to that of a killer shark or a serial killer. *Before the attack*, the enemy is silent. Conversely, a *test* is generally given by someone with whom you are familiar, someone you can trust, a teacher of some sort. *During the test*, the teacher is silent as well. The intent of the test is to determine how much of the lesson taught has been learned, so as to identify areas of strength, but more important, areas of weakness.

~

Whether we endure the test or simply survive the attack will depend on two critical factors: (1) how we define the experience and (2) the foundation on which our faith is built.

~

Satan does not attack a non-believer (a person who does not profess a faith in Jesus the Christ), because the non-believer is not his enemy. Satan's enemy is the believer (a person that professes a faith in Jesus the Christ). The strategy that satan uses against non-believers is to keep them blinded. He attempts to keep the non-believer from knowing the truth of God's Word and His promises. He uses the strategy of plucking up the seeds that are sown on hard soil. The truth is sown but the ground (of the heart) is not prepared to receive the seed. Satan's strategy against believers is to attempt to blindside them, manipulating believers with a distortion of the truth. He attempts to maneuver his way through the web of our emotions, in order to set up a "battlefield" in our minds.

What is the lesson to be learned from a "Job experience?" In life's journey, each of us will be confronted with something that may shake the foundation of our faith and the core of our being. The experience may challenge our health, wealth, or faith. Whether we endure the test or simply survive the attack will depend on two critical factors: (1) how we define the experience and (2) the foundation on which our faith is built.

If Job's faith had been counterfeit, his tragic experience would have destroyed him. But because Job loved and trusted God and sought to please Him, his faith enabled him to counter the fierce attack that satan waged against him. He was able to withstand this most difficult test. Because of God's grace and mercy, like Job, I survived my attack. But more important, I passed my test. Wisdom would not make room for me to curse God and die! But I found strength in Psalm 118:17 as I declared, again and again, "I will not die but live, and will proclaim what the Lord has done." I experienced the magnificence of God's excellence as I was entrusted into the gifted hands, intellect, and skill of my neurosurgeons and the operating room staff for eight hours. God healed me from the devastation of the brain tumor using the dedicated team of wonderful "ministers." Healing can be manifested in various ways: miraculously, using the gifts and skills of the traditional medical community or by use of naturopathic therapies that aid in the healing process. But I will state emphatically, that any way you look at it, healing is the sovereign act of God.

As Christians, we must by faith tap into the finished work of Jesus Christ on Calvary. Isaiah 53:5 says "But He (Jesus) was wounded and bruised for our sins. He was beaten that we might have peace; He was lashed and we were healed!" (TLB) This will allow us to exercise a *yadah* faith in God, knowing that provision has already been made for us to experience triumph over sickness, knowing that when we step out and appropriate that provision, "we *are* the healed." Despite any suffering we may experience, we must have an unquenchable faith that is not predicated on what we see. This resolve expresses a trust in the absolute power and control of God, regardless of what we experience between our prologue and our epilogue.

Insights from the Living Bible on "How Suffering Affects Us" [3]

Suffering is helpful when:

1. We turn to God for understanding, endurance, and deliverance.

2. We ask important questions we might not take time to think about in our normal routine.

3. We are prepared by it to identify with and comfort others who suffer.

4. We are open to be helped by others who are obeying God.

5. We are ready to learn from a trustworthy God.

6. We realize we can identify with what Christ suffered on the cross for us.

7. We are sensitized to the amount of suffering in the world.

Suffering is harmful when:

1. We become hardened and reject God.

2. We refuse to ask any questions and miss any lessons that might be good for us.

3. We allow it to make us self-centered and selfish.

4. We withdraw from the help others can give.

5. We reject the fact that God brings good out of calamity.

6. We accuse God of being unjust and perhaps lead others to reject [God].

7. We refuse to be open to any in our lives.

Chapter Five
My "Job-Like" Friends

———◦❦◦———

The cords of death entangled me; the torrents of destruction overwhelmed me ... In my distress I called to the Lord, I cried to my God for help.

Psalm 18:4–6 (KJV)

For four weeks after surgery, my family made a conscientious decision to limit my telephone calls and home visitations. Had this not been the case, my faith could have been challenged even more than it was by "naysayers" or "accusers" or misguided "well-wishers." There were some who attempted to help me "understand" what I was experiencing and why—some with good intent and some with questionable intent.

I am so grateful to God for the wisdom that my family exercised during this vulnerable period. Had they not shielded me from undue stress and irrelevant concerns, the process of my healing could have taken a different turn. It is God who provides healing to our bodies, but it is our responsibility to allow our bodies to be the sanctuary in which God's gift of healing can be manifested.

We read in the Book of Job about the ensuing visit of his friends: Bildad the Shuhite, Eliphaz the Temanite, Zophar the Naamathite, and Elihu the Buzite. They heard about Job's situation and came to comfort and console him. The Bible tells us, in Job 2, "they sat upon the ground with [Job] silently for seven days and nights, no one speaking a word; for they saw that [Job's] suffering was too great for words."

His friends did what was honorable, as they sought to bring comfort to Job. What went wrong during their visit was their attempt to explain God's thoughts and purpose.

In their attempt to try to defend heaven's honor,

> His three friends [explained to Job] that he must be suffering because of some terrible sin he committed. They [tried] to persuade Job to repent of his sin. When Job [argued] that he [had] not sinned enough to deserve such suffering, his friends [responded] with even harsher accusations. While there [were] elements of truth in the speeches of Job's friends, they [were] based on wrong assumptions. We must be careful what we assume to be true in the lives of others. We cannot assume that suffering is their fault or a result of their sin. (TLB) [4]

Each of Job's friends was operating in what I call EGO mode. EGO is my acronym for "Easing God Out." And as with Job's friends, sometimes our EGO misleads us into thinking we have answers to all of the whys and understand all of the wherefores in our lives and the lives of others. But in the fullness of time we are likely to be confronted with the reality that God is sovereign and has absolute power and control over all situations—and we know much of nothing!

God's sovereignty is not dictated by human actions or by human attempts to understand His action. The mind and movements of God are not limited to, nor restricted by, human thoughts or motion. God's sovereignty encompasses space, while we operate within the confines of that space. God's presence is eternal, while our earthly existence is time. God's wisdom is always and ever perfect while our understanding is in a continual process of learning. In Isaiah 55:8–9, God declares that:

my thoughts are not your thoughts, neither are your
ways my ways ... As the heavens are higher than the
earth, so are my ways higher than your ways and my
thoughts than your thoughts. (NIV)

Not only are there many revelations to gain from the study of the
bible, but there are also practical lessons. I often wonder which caused
Job the most distress: his personal tragedies or the emotional pain
inflicted upon him by his friends. While my family sheltered me from
visits by physical "Job-like" friends, I was, nonetheless, visited by my
own emotional friends. For seven metaphorical days and nights, these
emotional visitors sat with me—not one of them saying a word. But
when they finally did speak (to my mind), like Job, I was presented with
similar arguments.

I invite you to meet "them," so you'll know how to deal with
"imposters" in the midst of your own tests and trials.

Fanny Fear

My first emotional "Job-like" friend was Fanny Fear. During those
times when I felt alone and spiritually depleted, she would scream
in my ear, ever so loudly. I felt so overwhelmed. Her screams caused
me to lose my ability to discern what was going on, to hear God,
to keep my balance. My faith and my feelings of fear seemed to be
in a perpetual battle. And too often, it seemed as if Fanny Fear was
winning. Her ammunition appeared more powerful, more potent than
my shield of faith could deflect. Fanny kept confronting me with the
fact that the tumor was cancerous and could return. She assured me
that I would die.

The truth of the matter is that when our fear overtakes our faith in
God, we are operating in the realm of carnality. Romans 8:6–7 says:

...to be carnally minded [to have complete confidence
in one's feelings] is death: but to be spiritually minded

[to have a strong faith and belief in God] is life and peace … because the carnal mind is enmity [hatred; ill will; animosity] against God …

What we must keep in mind is that our faith in God will never demand a rational response to whatever is taking place. The ways of God are not logical, but they are perfect. In all this, *God said nothing.*

Danny Doubt

My second "friend," Danny Doubt, would tap me on my shoulder, awakening me in the wee hours of the morning. Even though Jerry lay close by my side and we slept hand-in-hand, Danny dared to invade the privacy and sanctity of our bedroom. He would argue with me, in the ear of my mind, with such deliberation that I often conceded. I was confused and afraid, but too ashamed to admit that after thirty-three years of relationship with the Lord, I was questioning: "God! Are You who You *say* You are?" At times, I felt alone, even though my husband was a breath away. And I continued the interrogation, "God, if You *are*, I need to know *where* You are and I need to know You have everything under control." *Still, God kept silent.*

~

I was confused and afraid, but too ashamed to admit that after thirty-three years of relationship with the Lord, I was questioning: "God! Are You who You say You are?"

~

Annie Anxiety

Annie Anxiety, my third "friend," was emphatic and insistent that my illness would eventually lead to death. The old cliché, "Everybody wants to go to heaven but nobody wants to die" became a tangible reality. By all accounts, the odds were stacked against me. The tumor was cancerous and the prognosis was that it could reoccur within four to five years. What caused me anxiety was *not* the immortal experience that takes place after physical death. As a Christian, I believe that when my spirit is absent from my body, I will be in the presence of the Lord (2 Corinthians 5:8). However, Annie insisted on exaggerating the physical *process* of dying. She painted a horrifying picture of me gasping for air, as I took my last breath. I had a severe bronchial attack once and I can vividly remember how frightening it was struggling for air—air that just seemed to tease my need to breathe. And the thought of being separated from my husband, leaving my children, and not being able to kiss and hug and know GiGi caused me to plead, *"Not now God, not now!"* Yet, God remained silent.

~

I prodded Him further, sarcastically, as I thought (without one iota of conviction), "God, I can quickly name at least ten people that I believe deserved a brain tumor and the anguish that I'm going through!"

~

Sammy Self-Pity

My fourth emotional "spokesman" was Sammy Self-Pity. During the middle of the night, when all else was quiet, Sammy would come and sit on my pillow. He stroked my head as he whispered ever so softly, "You don't deserve this punishment! Why did God allow this to happen to you?" Foolishly, I would agree with him as I questioned, "Yeah, Why me, God?" I prodded Him further, sarcastically, as I thought (without one iota of conviction), *God, I can quickly name at least ten people that I believe deserve a brain tumor and the anguish that I'm going through!* But God said nothing.

Alvin Anger

"It's not fair that you should die at such a young age. What did you do to deserve this?" my fifth "Job-like friend" growled. Mr. Anger prompted me to make an attempt to explain to God how much Jerry and I loved each other. As if He didn't already know.

"Our life is getting much easier now," I reasoned with God. "The children are grown and have become independent. I reminded God, asking, "What about the plans You gave me and Jerry for ministry? What about our new granddaughter? I've seen her, only, once! Doesn't she deserve to know me?" And I even threw in, "Doesn't she need me to tell her about the wonderful things You have done for our family?" Still nothing!

Charley Condemnation

Of all my "friends," it was Charley who brought me the greatest distress. His visits always left me with questions about my self-worth. "Do I mean much to you, God?" "Did I live a lie for the past thirty-three years?" "Was all this for nothing?" There were times when I was within a second of doubting the very *existence* of God. I felt like giving up on all I believed in. Not only was I angry that I could die and not enjoy the fullness of life, but I also felt condemned. Chuck most often left me with a sense of being unfit for God's use and service. I was left with a sheer sense of doom. God's silence was deafening.

Willie Wisdom

Willie Wisdom, my final "friend" kept silent all the while, until he finally spoke his piece. Everything with which the other six friends had inundated my mind, Willie was there to counter. Willie told me I had to use the power of remembrance. It was then that I began to recall the many miracles that God had performed for my family and me in the past. There were so many wonderful things that were constantly being stirred up in my thoughts. I could hear the sweet, soft melody of each memory in my ear—like a note to the score! But God's silence continued.

During this time, my faith in God was at war with my feelings of fear concerning the outcome of my illness. The battle was oxymoronic—bitter yet sweet. Although I was consumed with an internal conflict, simultaneously I was experiencing sweet, intimate, and precious moments with God. It seemed I was swirling around in the eye of a storm, yet I felt peace. I was confused in my mind, but my spirit was content. The best way I can describe myself during this period is feeling like that piece of fruit cocktail in a large bowl of Jell-O. Once fruit cocktail is set into Jell-O, regardless of how much the container is tossed about, it remains protected and intact. I was resting in God's sovereignty, amidst a world of confusion, but I knew (yadah) I was safe!

~

Quite frankly, I was afraid that acknowledging my feelings would negate my faith.

~

Knowing God's sovereignty and accepting my nothingness required me to acknowledge my feelings, even if it seemed to hinge on doubting my faith. Quite frankly, I was afraid that acknowledging my feelings would negate my faith. But nothing could be further from the truth! It is okay to experience emotions that make us feel vulnerable. After all, we are human.

Emotional wellness requires the ability to feel. When patients say they have no feeling about a situation or life experience...they have likely suppressed the feeling or dissociated from it because it is too painful...We need to be able to feel the range of emotions, from good to bad, to be healthy. When we have emotional freedom, we are able to experience our feelings and let go of them [and the accompanying fear]...Emotional freedom enables us to return to a states of peace and calm. [5]

There may be times when nothing seems to make sense and when life's situations become overbearing or overwhelming. In these critical moments, take your eyes off the status of your situation and look to God. He will give you a surefooted confidence as you trust Him. It is this confidence in God that will cause your faith to run like a deer across the rough and difficult terrain of life. I've come to understand that when my faith is combated by doubt, I need only to rest in my *covenant* with God, through Christ Jesus. Accepting God's sovereignty is not a head thing...it's a matter of the heart!

After crashing my "pity party," God spoke to me in a whirlwind and asked me some tough, but simple, questions:

Agnes, why do you **fear?** *Fear not [my child], for I am with you* (Isaiah 41:10).

Why the **doubt?** *Put your finger [by faith] into My hands. Put your hand into My side. Don't be faithless any longer. Believe in Me!* (John 20:27).

Why the **anxiety?** *Don't worry about anything; instead, pray about everything; tell God your need [and concerns], and don't forget to thank Him for His answers* (Philippians 4:6).

Why the **sorrow?** *[You have My promise that] all sorrow and all sighing will be gone forever; only joy and gladness will be there* (Isaiah 35:10).

My child, why the **anger?** *... When you are angry you give a mighty foothold to the devil* (Ephesians 4:27).

Why do you feel **condemned?** *... There is now no condemnation awaiting those who belong to Christ Jesus* (Romans 8:1).

Agnes, do not forget the counsel of **wisdom** *... Remember, remember, remember! Jesus Christ, the same, yesterday, today, and forever* (Hebrews 13:8).

I praise God not only for asking me the questions, but for giving me the answers.

Chapter Six
Trusting a Known God

————⚬⟊⟊⟊⟊⚬————

[I] cried out to God to help [me] and He did,
for [I] trusted in Him

I Chronicles 5:20 TLB

O n the morning of May 13, 1998 while resting in bed, I was startled by the shriek of the telephone. The call was from my sister-in-law, Geraldine. She was making her daily check-in call with me. During my recovery, it had become the norm to keep the radio in our bedroom tuned to an inspirational station at a low volume.

In the midst of telling Geraldine, "I'm all right. Everything is going pretty good," a barrel of tears began to flow. "I know God does not make mistakes," I told her through my sobs, "but ... but ... I just don't understand the purpose of what I'm going through." There I was, again, smack-dab in the middle of another "pity party." My precious sister-in-law prayed with me—expressing how much she wished she could come and spend some time with me. But I understood that her home responsibilities would not permit her to do so. As she continued talking with me, I was able to gather some peace and regain my composure. Before our conversation ended, she prayed with me, reminding me that everything was well. I truly appreciated her call, but just hearing her voice was a tease. If only I could be in her presence. I still felt confused and alone. But God knew best.

After she hung up, the radio's volume seemed to increase several decibels. It sounded as if the minister was actually standing in my bedroom with a microphone in hand: as if he knew where I was emotionally at that moment; as if he was given a special message just for me. He was talking about "the purpose for our suffering." His biblical reference was Philippians 1:12. I grabbed my bible from the nightstand and found the scripture, which reads, "...I [Paul] want you brothers and sisters to know that what has happened to me has helped to spread the good news." It is my belief that God allows us to experience distress in life so that our faith can be stretched. So that we (believers) may be bold to speak the gospel without fear in order that the unsaved (the unbeliever) might be saved. At that moment, I began to understand that this experience was my challenge! And that challenge was to "flesh out" what I had confessed that I believed over the years; to proclaim (to extol or praise publicly) that not only is Jesus Christ the Savior, but He is the healer!

The Reason for my Season

Since this experience, as I have mentioned, I have seen tremendous spiritual growth in the lives of many of my immediate and extended family members. Not only did the ordeal inspire change in the lives of my biological family members but many of my brothers and sisters in Christ have shared how my illness impacted their lives. Because my illness was so unexpected, they were challenged to evaluate the depth of their relationships with God. We must keep in mind that life is fragile and can change in the blink of an eye.

What this experience has taught me is that man cannot conceive or understand God's absoluteness and totality (His Sovereignty). God's actions are perfect even when our imperfect minds can make no sense of it all. God's actions in our lives have specific purposes (objectives) and authority (validity). Once we are able to embrace this understanding, we are on the pathway of knowing God's sovereignty as it relates to who we are.

This is Not about You!

May 14, 1998. I had recently watched the teaching video of a minister whose sermon was entitled "Anointing Jesus," and I was doing some follow-up study. As I read the story in the Gospels of the woman who anointed Jesus with expensive perfume, the Spirit of God began to speak to me, in a most profound and assuring way.

After reading the account in Matthew 26:6–13, I proceeded to the referred text in Mark 14:3–9, then to Luke 7:36–46, and finally to John 11:2. I noticed in the book of John that the text was subtitled, "Lazarus becomes ill and dies." Thinking that I had misread the reference, I turned back to Luke and confirmed that the referred text was correct.

This text identified the woman (referred to in Matthew and Mark) as Mary, the sister of Martha and Lazarus. However, there was no further mention of her anointing Jesus. I continued reading John 11:2–4:

> Well, her brother Lazarus, who lived in Bethany
> with Mary and her sister Martha, was sick.
> So the two sisters sent a message to Jesus telling him,
> "Sir, your good friend is very, very sick."
> But when Jesus heard about it he said, "The purpose of his
> illness is not death, but for the glory of God. I, the
> Son of God, will receive glory from this situation (TLB)

As I read verse 4, my spirit quickened (agreed) as the Spirit of God spoke, "Agnes, your sickness is not unto death, but that I am glorified; that my Son, Jesus, will receive glory in this experience. This is not about you!" I was the vessel that God chose to use. And with that, I was engulfed by an unexplainable peace; a sweet settling of my uneasiness. At that precise moment, I experienced "a place with God" unlike anywhere I had ever been. Finally, the Spirit began to give me answers to my "whys." This scripture (John 11:4) made clear to me that this experience would be a testimony to others of the miraculous healing power of God.

I was reminded of the divine strategies and interventions God provided for me during this experience. It was God that prompted Jerry to come up from the basement on March 20 at 11:15 pm. If he had not been upstairs at the time I experienced the seizures, it is likely that I could have died from asphyxiation or suffocation. It was God that intercepted the ambulance, causing their rapid response to Jerry's call to 911.

It was God that caused Geraldine to ask Bettye and Terry to come be with Jerry while he was in the Emergency Room. Bettye's extensive hospital experience prompted her to question whether I was "bucking" the respirator. It was God that "assigned" one of the operating room nurses to minister to me by laying her hand on me, as I waited outside the operating room. She prayed the prayer of faith over me, the surgeons, the anesthesiologist, and the ancillary operating-room staff, before I was taken into surgery. I can still recall her petition to God on my behalf. "Dear God...let there not be room for one smidgen of error during the surgery..." as I drifted into a sweet and peaceful rest.

It was God that took me through eight hours of surgery to remove the brain tumor on Monday, March 30. After my surgery, I stayed in the recovery room overnight. Because my stay in Recovery was unremarkably "divine," there was not justification to be transferred to the Intensive Care Unit (as is typical after a craniotomy). Rather, I was transferred to the Step-Down Unit (a specialty level of care between intensive care and a regular bed). I progressed, quickly, from a liquid diet for breakfast to a regular diet by dinner on Tuesday. By late Wednesday afternoon, I had received medical clearance from my cardiologist, ophthalmologist, and physical therapist.

It was God that gave wisdom to the neurosurgeon and his team to believe and conclude that they had removed the entire cancerous tumor. Therefore, neither chemotherapy nor radiation therapy was recommended. Jerry and I consulted, later, with an oncologist, at another major medical center in New York for a second opinion.

That oncologist did a study of the operative report and had an independent pathological study of the tumor cells done. He concurred with my neurosurgeon's decision that I not be administered radiation and/or chemotherapy treatments. Hallelujah to Almighty God!

It was God that caused me to recover so speedily from the trauma and surgery. Three days after undergoing the craniotomy to remove the brain tumor, I was discharged and *walked* out of the hospital on Thursday. And I have not stopped running, leaping, and jumping, full of gratitude to God. It was God who strengthened and restored health to my body, allowing me to return to work full-time in July, as a school nurse.

The events that took place between "our" decision to have surgery up until I regained consciousness in the recovery room are very vague in my memory. But according to Jerry, I was actively engaged in all of the discussions and decisions made regarding my surgery. About a year after the surgery, I was clearing up some of the paperwork clutter from my hospital stay and I came across the Health Care Proxy form that I don't even remember signing! It was God that gave me the mental ability to participate in the decision-making process regarding my surgery. At the same time, it was God that shielded me from the emotional trauma of this event. Miraculously, I came back to my sense of awareness with an intimate knowing of God's sovereignty.

The Pocono Experience

On numerous occasions, our dear friends Elliot and Kathy have graciously shared God's bountiful blessings with us. So naturally, after the surgery, they lovingly extended an invitation for us to visit with them at their home in the Poconos. They knew we needed a little rest and relaxation, so upon our arrival, they gave us the keys to their guesthouse. The beds were nice and fluffy and the cupboards were filled to capacity with lots of goodies. Their video and CD shelves would have given the audio/video sections at Blockbuster and Walmart some serious competition. "Call us if you need us," were their final instructions as they left.

In the early morning hours of June 27, 1998, for whatever reason, we were unable to sleep. And as Jerry and I were talking, we thought we heard a noise downstairs. I'm sure I don't have to tell you that we were scared stiff. It was pitch dark in the Poconos, and needless to say, Jerry was in no hurry to go downstairs and investigate. But "my bashert" eventually mustered enough nerve to go down and see what was going on. Finding all to be well, Jerry called out for me to join him in the living room. Since we were wide awake, we decided to get a snack and watch television. When I turned on the TV, a well-known healing ministry program was already in progress on Trinity Broadcasting Network. At the end of the broadcast, the minister stretched out his hands and asked those in the television audience who were sick to come and touch the screen as a point of contact. Ordinarily, I would not have gotten up, but this time I felt *compelled* to touch the screen—so I placed my hands over the minister's hands.

Just the day before, we'd watched a video tape of Bishop T.D Jakes. Bishop Jakes shared that sometimes when we exercise faith, it requires us to do things that are not *common,* that may seem stupid. And yes, I felt mighty stupid at the thought of placing my hands on the TV screen as I complied with the minister's request. My actions were so "not me" as I hesitantly stood up. But James 2:17 informs us that "faith by itself, if it is not accompanied by action, is dead." At the time, it seemed a rather benign act. But when my hands "met" Pastor Benny Hinn's, he immediately said, "Someone that's touching the screen has just been healed from the effects of a brain tumor." I screamed, "*That's me ... by faith!*" Jerry and I looked at each other in total amazement. The sound was as if my voice had come from someone or somewhere else.

In retrospect, the thought that God would allow us to come to the Poconos, awaken us from our sleep at 1:45 am, and draw us to a healing ministry broadcast in order that I make a point of contact is still amazing! I am reminded of the woman who had suffered with an issue of bleeding for twelve years. All of the other remedies she tried had failed. But as she warily pressed her way through the crowd of people and touched the hem of Jesus' garment, she received her healing. And just like that woman pressed in with her faith, my "point of contact faith" compelled God to respond on my behalf. All it really takes is—just one touch!

Just Trust Me

Friday, May 22, Jerry and I attended the "Sweet Sixteen" party of our niece, Courtney. It was my first time out in a large crowd since the surgery. I was so excited, as a matter of fact, rather sassy! I circulated quite a bit during the evening chatting with family and old friends. They could hardly believe how rapidly and graciously I was recovering. What an enjoyable time we had!

Saturday morning, I woke up about eight o'clock and attempted to get out of bed to go to the bathroom. I can still recall my legs feeling unusually heavy. I thought the weighted feeling was related to my standing more than usual the night before. As I got out of bed, I looked down at my legs and was terrified at what I saw. The flesh on both my thighs had fallen down over my knees, like the fold on an elephant's leg. Panic set in and tears began to race down my face.

I did not want Jerry to see this, so I struggled to the bathroom on my own. I could barely raise myself up from the commode because my legs were weak and wobbly. Instead, I turned and knelt down on the side of the commode and cried out to God for help. "God, I can't lose the gift of healing you've given me! I can't, I just can't!" I stayed beside the commode, crying and praying, for a little while. Then, I struggled down to the basement (two levels), ignorantly hoping that exercise might help. This was a blatant disregard of my neurosurgeon's specific instructions *not* to engage in any unattended exercise. Straddling the stationary bicycle, I peddled, prayed and cried; peddled and prayed and cried.

A short time later, I heard Jerry's footsteps coming downstairs. Once he saw what I was doing, he chastised me. "Agnes," he asked sternly, "Why are you exercising down here alone? What were the doctor's instructions?" Not wanting to share my reasoning, I timidly responded, "I'm just exercising a little." He scolded me and said, "Well, you just get off that bike and let's go right back upstairs." I obliged, but as I got off the bike, I became hysterical, showing him my thighs. Jerry gasped and pointed, saying, "Sit down on that ottoman!"

During our marriage, it was very seldom that Jerry demonstrated anger. But that morning, he turned and took the stairs two by two. I knew a war was inevitable. He was back downstairs in record time and started to anoint (rub) me with oil. As he prayed the prayer of faith for my healing, he began to massage my legs and thighs gently. But then, each stroke became firmer and more deliberate. It was sort of the way I remembered my mother kneading dough for her delicious biscuits.

As he continued massaging, the authoritative voice of the Holy Spirit began to speak through Jerry, in an unknown language. The Spirit prayed through him according to Romans 8:26: "Likewise the [Holy] Spirit also helpeth our infirmities [weakness]: for we know not what we should pray for as we ought: but the [Holy] Spirit … maketh intercession for us with groanings which cannot be uttered" (KJV).

As God's presence filled the atmosphere, Jerry was slain in the Spirit. He fell to the floor, backward. The form of his body was like that of a cross. His arms were stretched out straight, perpendicular to his body, and his legs were stuck together, as if they were glued. His eyes were fastened heavenward.

As I watched the move of God, in awe, I knew that the *Shikenah Glory*, God's presence, had filled our basement that morning. Soon afterward, the Holy Spirit released, through me, the interpretation of the utterance that Jerry had just spoken. And this is the Word of God that came forth: "Just trust me! Just trust me! I want you to know Me in the power of My might!" Then I was lifted off of the ottoman on which I was sitting, landing right next to Jerry on the floor.

The Spirit of God continued to speak through me—to me—etching His Word in my mind and spirit. "Haven't I taken care of you in the past? Haven't I healed your sickness and disease in the past? Haven't I extended my love to you? I will continue to care for you. I am your God and I will continue to heal you. Get to know Me! Get to know Me! Get to know Me!"

The second and third admonitions were louder and even more emphatic than the first. Then a sweet silence settled on Jerry and me as we lay on our basement floor and waited before God. Once we sensed God's presence had lifted, we witnessed the miraculous work of God. As I stood up, we noticed that my thigh muscles that had folded over my knees were now firmly in place, as they were supposed to be! Our God is the awesome God. Our God can be trusted.

I must continue pressing on to keep my healing in the midst of the enemy's attack. You may one day need to do the same. It is a sacred and delicate time when you are recovering from a traumatic experience. During this period, you must be intimate with the Lord as never before, to allow Him to restore (heal) and comfort you: body, soul and spirit. One example I can use to illustrate this is the nature of my relationship with Jerry, before and after marriage. I knew (yada) Jerry during our friendship, courtship, and before our marriage; but after the consummation of our marriage, I know (yadah) him intimately.

And so it must be at such a crucial time in your relationship with God; there are just some things that only you and your Lover can experience *alone.*

> Through it all, through it all
> I've learned to trust in Jesus
> I've learned to trust in God
> Through it all, through it all
> I've learned to depend on His Word
> —Andrae Crouch

Chapter Seven
A Scar of Remembrance

———⚬❦⚬———

He did this so ... that all the people of the earth might know the hand of the Lord, that it is mighty: that ye might fear the Lord your God forever.

Joshua 4:24

"*Mirror, mirror on the wall,*" I thought one day, as I stood staring at myself in the bathroom, "*will I ever be fair again?*" The location of the tumor was on the left frontal lobe of my brain, and the surgery had left me with a three-inch scar and a quarter-inch indentation on my scalp and forehead. So often while washing my face, I would question, "Why am I left with this scar?" I didn't like having a visible reminder of this harrowing experience.

I can remember telling Tracey a few years earlier that when I turned fifty I would cut all of my hair off and stop wearing bras. She responded, "Why are you going to get stupid when you turn fifty?" Obviously, the Holy Spirit and Jerry had a lot to do with my not carrying out the latter of my plan, but it seemed as if I had spoken something into existence. Needless to say, the scar on my forehead and the "forced" haircut *did* affect my self-image.

As I continued to question, "Why the scar?" the Spirit of God brought to my remembrance the story of how the children of Israel crossed the

Jordan River and entered Canaan on dry land (Joshua 3,4). After the crossing, God commanded that twelve men (one from each tribe) carry twelve stones from the Jordan and lay them in a pile on the shore in Gilgal as a monument. *Gilgal* means to end, to remove the reproach of Egypt from off you. God told them that this monument would serve as a memorial (a sign), so that when their children asked, "What do these stones mean?" "You will answer ... the Lord your God dried up the waters of Jordan from before you, until [you] passed over ... that all the people ... might know the hand of the Lord, that it is mighty: that ye might fear the Lord your God for ever." (Joshua 4:23, 24).

Suddenly, the significance of the scar on my forehead became clear. As a matter of fact, it was very obvious. It is to serve as a sign to me of God's sovereignty, of God's absolute power. It is to serve as a memorial to my children and my children's children and to all people that they might know that the hand of God continues to be mighty; that we might fear the Lord our God forever!

Crossing the Jordan seemed impossible to the children of Israel and often, many of us face "impossible river crossings" in our lives. Your impossible experience may be an illness, feeling trapped in an abusive relationship or marriage, being entangled in the grip of an addiction, or any number of circumstances. The ability to cross over any of these may seem impossible. But with God's help, you can overcome the obstacles of life so that you can camp in "Gilgal" on the way to your "Promised Land" of purpose.

When Israel camped in Gilgal, the pitched stones were a constant reminder to them and their children of the mighty act God had performed on their behalf. It was there that circumcision was performed, again, after almost thirty-nine years (only the second time since they left Egypt). Sometime, in our lives, we must "set up camp" to allow God to circumcise our hearts of excess and unclean flesh. If these "filthy" areas are not removed from our heart, they will fester and spread. This purulence will create an unhealthy environment, a place where the sins of malice, envy, and every evil work can harbor and lead to more systemic maladies. We must, also, observe our own form of circumcision by offering ourselves to God as a clean vessel for His use. If we don't circumcise our hearts, minds, and emotions, we will constantly relive the traumatic experiences of the past. This will require us to return to our Gilgal. You may feel you've removed the "foreskin" of your experience. But ask any parent of an uncircumcised boy—they will attest that there can be a lot of "junk" remaining between the folds. Neglecting to focus on the area where the bacteria breed will cause one to carry an offensive odor. So let us be sure to pull back the "folds" and expose the junk!

During one of my visits with Arnold and his family, GiGi (who was three at the time) was sitting on my lap. We were having one of our "I love you and you are so beautiful" talks. As GiGi cupped my face in her hands, she questioned, "Nana, why do you have that hole on your head?" sticking her little finger in the indentation. Holding back tears, I told her as much as I felt she could understand at the time.

Every year, our family celebrates "the miracle of March 20" and the scar remains a memorial to us. Now that GiGi is older, she has come to know more of the intimacies of Nana's illness and healing and she (and her little sister, Lai Lei) understand now that the hand of God continues to be monumental.

"We Celebrate Life!"

Thanks to the Holy Spirit and Jerry's insistence, I still wear bras, but I love my new-found freedom ... *my natural hairstyle.* I count it a privilege to wear the scar and indentation on my forehead. It serves as a constant reminder of the mighty act that God performed on my behalf.

> Mirror, mirror on the wall
> Who is blessed above them all?
> When the events of '98 I recall
> Then on my knees, I always fall.
> When I look in the mirror
> This is what I see
> No one but miracle
> Looking back at me.
> —Rance Allen

Epilogue
My Story, God's Glory

———⊷❈⊶———

Things that I've gone through in my life
I thought were too hard for me, for me to bear
But I remember reading in God's Word
Where He said He would not put more on me than I can bear
Yes, Jesus cares, and all I've endured was only for my good

—LaShaun Pace

More than twelve years have passed since that fateful day in March 1998. The storm has passed over—Hallelujah! I survived the attack, but more importantly, *I passed the test.* There are life situations that still attempt to challenge my knowing God faith. But because of the experience, my response time to answering the question "who God is" gets quicker with each challenge. My faith in the sovereign acts of God has been tried and purified through the fires of life. I know God in greater measure, and in larger dimension.

So much has happened since my healing from cancer. Today, Jerry and I are retired from our professional careers in New York and have relocated to the Southland. Jerry is now Pastor Jerry and I am Elder Agnes. We, along with our children, Arnold, Tracey, and Doneisha are actively involved in developing a church ministry, "Perfecting the Heart Worship Center" in Chester, South Carolina.

"REACHING THE MASSES!"

Ever so often, I will discuss with Jerry the events of 1998, trying to gain insight. It was early one morning in 2003 that God allowed me a visualization of how He preserved and restored me from what *could* have been the devastation of my life.

The night before, we had just concluded a wonderful bible study at church when one of our elders suddenly took ill. EMS rushed her to the hospital. She underwent emergency surgery and was subsequently placed on life support. Unfortunately, she did not recover and the decision was made to disconnect her from life support.

After her family and our pastors spent time with her, Jerry and I were allowed to visit her bedside. As I stood and looked at our dear sister's bloated and distorted body, oozing fluid from every crevice, I was in total disbelief that this was the same woman who was ministering just twelve hours before. As Jerry and I said our "good-byes," Jerry whispered gently in my ear, "Agnes, you looked more horrific in March 1998 than she does right now." I was in shock, to say the least, yet full of gratitude to God for gracing me with life.

For my sixtieth birthday in 2006, Jerry and I took a Mediterranean cruise along with some of our friends in New York: Sharon, Ariel, "Mom Rita," and Lorna. Over the years, we have cruised six times with this particular cruise line. As a result, we have forged a great relationship. As a matter of fact, the relationship with the cruise line has afforded us some wonderful upgrades on several trips. Though we traveled five times before with this particular cruise line, something quite peculiar occurred which made us a bit uncomfortable this time.

At one of the ports in the Mediterranean, cruise passengers were required to leave their passports with the cruise-line staff before disembarking at port for the day. At first, Jerry and I felt uneasy and decided that we didn't want to take that risk. But there was one site, in particular, that we really wanted to visit. And our passports were the only things we had that could prove who we were. After some thought and prayer, we made the decision that we would trust this cruise line to be our "sovereign protection" while we were touring in that foreign country. So we cautiously surrendered our passport because we "trusted them." This trust was based on confidence in the relationship we had developed with the cruise line over the years.

And to you, my dear reader, so it is with God! The mighty liner of God's sovereign design continues to keep its steady course over the sea of history. God moves us undisturbed and unhindered toward the fulfillment of the eternal purposes which He ordained for us in Christ Jesus before the world began. We do not know all that is included in these purposes, but enough has been disclosed to furnish us with a broad outline of things to come and to give us good hope and firm assurance of our future well-being.

I Corinthians 13:12 tells us that "we can only see and understand a little about God now, as if we were peering at his reflection in a poor mirror. But someday we are going to see Him in His completeness, face to face. Now all that I know is hazy and blurred, but then I will see everything clearly, just as clearly as God sees in my heart right now. (TLB)

Yet Another Reason

If you think GiGi is "yummy yummy," just know that our second granddaughter, Laila Leigh (our sweet "Lai Lei bug), is "bubblelicious!"

Laila, your birth not only brought joy to our family on May 11, 2002, but you are yet another reason I know (in my knower) that God allowed me to remain on planet Earth. You, also, needed to know me and most assuredly, I needed to know you. I want you to know also that the hand of God continues to be monumental. Nana Agnes loves you so much!

An Invitation

Thank you for sharing this time with me. I may never know why you decided to read this book, but I'm grateful to have made your acquaintance. I've enjoyed your company. You've traveled with me during one of the most profound segments of my life's journey.

At times, if you didn't notice, it seemed as if I was confronted with insurmountable variances: signs that read "Detour," "Roadway Narrowing—Watch out for oncoming traffic," and "Caution —Shift in gradient." There's one I'm sure you did not miss: "Slow down—God at work." During this journey, the very core of my being (spirit, soul, and body) was challenged to make a "forever commitment" to the authority of the sovereign God. Frankly, maneuvering the course was not only tedious, but extremely tiring at times. But when I became aware that God was controlling the "traffic flow," I was able to release the anxiety and stress.

Because you chose to spend this time with me, I am concerned about you. How are things going, my friend? Where are you located on your spiritual journey? We may never meet in person, but I wish above all else that you will come to know the Sovereign God through His Son, Jesus Christ. If you have not yet made that commitment and desire to do so, I encourage you to pray this simple prayer now:

> Lord Jesus, I acknowledge that I have sinned
> in my thoughts, words, and actions. I ask

Your forgiveness. I invite You to come into
my heart and cleanse me from all unrighteousness.
Be my Lord and Savior and lead me on the
path of righteousness. Amen

If you have made this commitment to Jesus Christ, you are now a Christian—a "child of God." The bible instructs in John 3:17 that "God did not send His Son [Jesus] into the world to condemn it, but to save it" (TLB). I encourage you to read your bible and pray, daily. Find a church where you can grow in your faith in Jesus Christ.

I expect you see you in heaven! Please make my acquaintance.

References

1. A. W. Tozer, *The Knowledge of the Holy* (New York, NY: Harper and Row Publishers, 1961) p. 118.
2. Mart DeHaan, *The Great Debate, The People vs. Job* (RBC Ministries-News and Comments, January 2001)
3. Insights on "How Suffering Affects Us", *Life Application Bible* (Tyndale House Publishers, Inc., Wheaton, Ill. 60189, 1988) p. 807.
4. *Three Friends Answer Job* (Commentary, Life Application Bible) p. 782.
5. Dr. Andrea D. Sullivan, *A Path To Healing* (Doubleday, New York, 1998) p. 45.

Breinigsville, PA USA
28 September 2010
246276BV00002B/1/P